SO YOU THINK YOU'RE A
HIPSTER?

DOG 'n' BONE

Kara Simsek

with illustrations by Paul Parker

SO YOU THINK YOU'RE A HIPSTER?

Cautionary case studies from the city streets

First published in 2013 by Dog 'n' Bone Books

This edition published in 2017 by Dog 'n' Bone Books
An imprint of Ryland Peters & Small Ltd
20–21 Jockey's Fields   341 E 116th Street
London WC1R 4BW   New York, NY 10029

www.rylandpeters.com

10 9 8 7 6 5 4 3 2 1

A CIP catalog record for this book is
available from the Library of Congress
and the British Library.

ISBN: 978 1 911026 17 4

Editor: Pete Jorgensen
Design: Wide Open Studios
Illustration: Paul Parker

Printed in China

Introduction 6

The Hipsters

INTRODUCTION

What happened to your local area? Where did all these twenty-somethings in beanies and ripped skinny jeans come from? Why does the air hang thick with the foul stench of soya milk lattes and organic cupcakes?

What are these strange bikes with brightly colored frames and no brakes? Why is everyone walking a pug or carrying a freshly baked rye baguette under their arm?

How can there be twelve graphic-design agencies based in one building? What the hell is a pop-up organic burrito truck? How does that girl make a living from DJing when she just plays an iPod at a dingy bar once a week? Who are these people protesting against globalization as they Instagram photos of each other messing around on skateboards?

Sounds like you've woken up to find your neighbourhood transformed in to a hipster ghetto.

Want to have a night out? Your option is warehouse party,

warehouse party, or fanzine fundraiser... in a warehouse. Don't need glasses? No worries, just pretend, everyone else is. Not worn that sweater since you were ten? Put it on. No longer can you buy a pint of Heineken at the local bar, it's craft beers only. Say hello to Blueberry Ale and Williamsburg Hop Pilsner, and prepare your tastebuds for locally sourced tomato juice in your Saturday morning Bloody Mary. You like scotch eggs now they've been made by an organic artisan who trained in France.

Try and fit in. Wear something outrageous when shopping for groceries (at local retailers only, big-name supermarkets are a no-no), start a blog, get a specific interest that allows you to sit comfortably and look down on everyday people that know nothing about art-house cinema from the 1970s or thrash bands from New York state, who can't tell the difference between Flaubert and Baudelaire. Tell people you're relocating to Scandinavia to design eco-furniture and live off the land. To fish and knit and blog and be free from the constraints of Capitalism and the big city.

Remember, you're better than everyone else. And you're NOT a hipster. Labels are so lame. And you're better than that.

THE URBAN HUNTER.

The all-weather, all-action city woodsman, at one with nature. He even caught a mouse once.

Dave felt five pairs of eyes linger on him as he pulled up his boxers. The wood-paneled walls greedily absorbed the small slice of light that filtered through the half-open curtains. There was no movement in the room other than the shuffle of a slightly overweight man searching for his socks.

The eyes continued to stare. A trout kept company by a sad-looking sprig of time-withered seaweed; a stoat embroiled in a never-ending battle with a snake; a mangy crow on a half-broken plinth; a shabby stag's head. His small room was abundant with hunting trophies inherited from his grandad.

He breathed in sharply as he forcefully closed the button fly of his jeans. He'd been over-indulging on craft beers again. "But locally brewed ale just tastes so much better," he mused. Relaxing, he felt the weight of his gut fall against the solid waistband; the dense forest of hair that engulfed his midriff kept safe from the pinching denim by the thick twill of his red plaid shirt.

He gazed at himself in the mirror. Every button—from his collar to his crotch—was secured. The small white buttons on the two chest pockets and at the end of each long sleeve were also in place. A hint of his Casio digital watch could be seen peeping from below the left cuff. It caught the light, flashing silver as he reached down to tie the laces of his Red Wing work boots.

He was almost ready to venture outside. He stroked his full beard thoughtfully, enjoying the texture of the coarse hairs. It was his proudest achievement. Never before had he dedicated so much time to a project, and it was worth all the effort. He turned and weakly groped for his woolen hat; light brown in color it was hard to distinguish from the peaks and troughs of his unmade bed. He found it and, after running his thick, hairy fingers through his long, knotted hair, pulled it over his head, taking care to ensure it hid his receding hairline. His outfit made him ready for the worst the day could throw at him.

The stairs creaked beneath his bulk as he made his way to the front door. Opening it, he was bathed in sunlight as another August day began. He squinted as he headed to the design studio, where he would spend the next eight hours alternating between messing about on Photoshop and looking at obscure Japanese film trailers on YouTube.

FIXIE FIEND

The red-light renegade who fears no car... until he hits one whilst running a light.

I told my parents I wanted a new bike for Christmas. All my friends have them, and I was getting sick of running alongside them, carrying the cider. And besides, brogues aren't really designed for jogging along Hackney's uneven pavements. I was so fucked off this one time, I scuffed my coolest pair of shoes—they were Church's, conker-brown patent leather—and then some mayonnaise from a discarded box of chicken got in the scuff and... I was bummed. But that's living in a city for you.

Christmas came and I was back with the folks in Suffolk. I couldn't wait to get back to London. My friend was putting on a Boxing Day warehouse rave called "Gold, Frankinsence, and Merk." The flyer was so sick, it had a picture of the nativity, and below the Wise Men it said "Magi Lazer." So funny.

When it came to opening the presents, my parents handed me an envelope. I thought they were giving me a note saying "the present that you got us was shit," as when they opened it, they looked really bemused. I thought they'd like it, but it turns out they're not in to that kind of photography. Guess I'm on a different cultural plane since I moved to London.

There were actually two hundred notes in the envelope—cash for my bike! Fuck, I was so happy. Straight away I was looking at my favourite bike blog, Prolly Is Not Probably, to get ideas for my special ride. Now I was more determined than ever to get back to London, I needed to get my wheels ASAP.

A visit to Tokyo Fixed bike shop left me distraught, the cheapest bike they did was a grand. I felt like Santa had totally fucked me over and his elves were toying with me. What was I going to do with two hundred sheets? I was about to call my dealer when I saw the most beautiful bike. It had a shiny blue frame, black leather seat, and a yellow aerospoke wheel—it looked a bit like one of the bikes my mates rode, but it had brakes! No need to peddle backwards! Best of all, it was only £200!

Heading home, I felt like I had lost my virginity all over again. We caressed every bump in the road as her delicate frame shuddered against the rough tarmac. I touched the space between her handlebars gently. My buttocks on her plump seat felt just right. The way riding fixed really connects you with the road is so beautiful. Being at one with your machine is exhilarating. I swelled with pride as I watched her tyres transform from virginal white to café crème to dirty brown as we powered, harder and faster, along the cycle paths to London Fields.

I don't lock my bike up—it's too precious to be left alone. If I go to get chicken after we've been at a club, the bike comes too. Some nights I just cycle through Dalston; I love parading down "The Strip." I know most of the people who work at the best bars, so if I wanna go in I just cycle straight through the doors, they're cool with it. They know what it's like to ride fixed. It's a unique bond. You wouldn't leave your really hot girlfriend chained up outside a club, would you?

CONTEMPORARY ARTIST

"My name is Gunther von Gunther von Gagstein. And they say that since I moved to Berlin, it has been a much quieter place."

He raised one arm up from beneath his cape and made a slow gesture from floor to ceiling. The walls were lined with hundreds of pairs of staring eyes—staring at each other, staring at the floor, staring upon the shaven-headed man standing below them. The room resembled an amphitheatre of death.

Gunther, or GvGvG, as he is referred to by the arts press, used his collection of dead animals for one of three reasons: friendship, taxidermy, or blood letting. The latter was his favorite. Just recently he'd finished a large 10 by 8 meter canvas that he'd painted using a mixture of crow and fox blood.

"Each species' haemoglobin congeals in a different way," he explained. "The crow's is more aerated due to its life of flight. And the fox's dries with a fur-like texture because it eats rabbits and rats." He dreams of cutting off a man's penis and using it as a paintbrush. "I fantasize it would be like one of those washing-up sponges that you can fill with liquid soap," he sniggered. "Or a potato stamp!"

GvGvG's other favorite medium is taxidermy. "People say I

want to play God," he mused, gently stroking one of his creations—a pheasant with a rat's head and gold-plated talons. "And to those volk I say, '*Ja, das ist richtig*!' It was after I saw *Terminator 2* that I became possessed with the need to distil living creatures and then reblend them. Nature is ugly, I make it interesting and compelling!" A rabbit wearing a monocle and a codpiece looks on, making eye contact with the stuffed black crow perched on Gunther's arm.

The artist has sold none of his work—despite huge bids from collectors. He is adamant that none of his art will leave his care until he is dead. Only then can the entire lot be sold to the highest bidder, but his bloody artworks and reworked creatures will still be under his watchful gaze. "I will join them in an eternity of death," he yelps. "I will become the Christ figure in their Nativity scene!"

So the rumors are true. GvGvG's assistants will remove his hands, feet, and face, then work them into his most extreme piece yet. "There is a bear in Berlin zoo that I know to be very sick," he says. "It is to his body that my extremities and visage will be sewn. Like the berserker of Nordic folklore I will haunt and terrorize my enemies."

DRUGS BORE

Drug addicts don't take drugs to get high, they take them to function. The drugs bore takes them to make his mundane life seem that bit more interesting.

For the drug addict, shuffling from the bed to the kettle to make a morning cup of coffee sometimes requires a line for propulsion. The scraping noise of a credit card against a dinner plate is a welcome relief from the shrill chimes of an alarm clock. Buying drugs from these people is a notoriously long process. If you go to their place, they might be too paranoid to let you in, or they might be too comatose to even hear the knock at the door. Maybe you'll turn up and discover your friendly local dealer is now under the control of a crack-whore who has hiked up the prices to maximize profits. These factors can all put a downer on your plans for the night.

However, people who take drugs because they think they're part of an important cultural movement are far more irritating than the addict/dealer who might be too high to sell you a gram of ketamine for your night out. They infiltrate house parties, clubs, and bars, holding court with a gaggle of like-minded fuckheads, people who have lost their friends and don't want to be stood outside chain-smoking hoping to spot them, and drugs vultures—the kind of people who will guffaw and feign shock at anything if it means getting offered a free line or two.

The drugs bore is easily distinguished by his loud voice, which he deems ideal for telling everyone the amount of mescaline he recently consumed at an art gallery opening. If someone innocently asks what that is, the drugs bore's face will curl into an incredulous sneer. "You don't know what mescaline is? Wow. It's a hallucinogen, it's pretty hardcore, you probably wouldn't be able to handle it," he'll say, grinning and shaking his head simultaneously; his eyes squeezed into a reptilian slit.

As the night progresses, the drugs bore will show off his unstoppable appetite for narcotics. "Give me a line of that," "Let's split this pill, it's a 2CB and MDMA mix," "Do you want to put some coke in my joint?" until he is not much more than a pair of rolling eyes set in a concrete jaw.

His original brags of being "so high" and how he is like a narcotic MacGyver— able to fashion a crack pipe out of any three household items—are forgotten as he trips up, trips over, and trips out. "Oh my god, that nitrous balloon has totally fucked me," he'll mutter, his hand limply holding the flaccid inflatable and his nose burned from amyl nitrate. He ensures all eyes are on him as he starts seeing faces rise up from stained carpets, or talks to people that only he can see.

ON FACIAL HAIR

For a time, it seemed to be en vogue for male hipsters to dress like someone who had mild learning difficulties.

It wasn't uncommon to see a man queuing patiently for his soy latte wearing an oversized anorak, an ill-fitting patterned jumper, and jeans that were three inches too short. Those really dedicated to the look might even rock battered sneakers and graying sports socks. The thick-framed glasses, regardless of whether they had prescription lenses or not, were the icing on the greasy-haired cake. But, as this style began to cement itself into the mainstream, the movers and shakers realized they had to do something to distinguish themselves from those who had bought the components required to achieve the look from a shopping mall. They also needed to distance themselves from those who actually dressed slightly off-kilter, because these people were perhaps not the sharpest tools in the box.

Their answer was to grow moustaches and, suddenly, the streets of east London and Williamsburg were awash with men who resembled tabloid E-fits of pedophiles. It was never clear who did it first, but soon it was more likely to see a man with a moustache than not. Pencil, bushy, waxed, patchy, unkempt, groomed, long, short, handlebar—no one style was better than another. And each one was tended to with utmost dedication by the super-cool "creative" who had cultivated it.

Interestingly, the moustache remained, even after the majority abandoned the "I sit in a bus station all day" look. It worked just as well—better, some might even argue—with a pair of smart chinos and a checked shirt. In the right light, the glossy waxed curl of a 'tache could set off the sheen of a smart pair of brogues perfectly. Straight-faced graphic designers, who live and breathe such minor aesthetics, embraced the look whole-heartedly.

There was really only one problem with the moustache—it looked repulsive, especially on ginger people. It made it harder for men to attract girls. A line of hair above a man's lips can mean "Magnum PI," but on the other hand it can also mean "John Waters." How was a woman to differentiate?

Many men were left out of pocket after a night out. Broke and alone, a man would rue the hours spent chatting up a girl, only to be met with a surprised utterance of "You're not gay?" as he moved in for a kiss. Similarly, many gay guys were left aghast that the cute guy with the great ass, 'tache, and low-cut vest was eyeing up their fag-hag friend and not them.

Unsurprisingly, the full beard began to take over as the facial hair option of choice for hipsters. Still bad news for gingers, but for the average lusty young hipster, the only obstacle he'll now face is convincing women that he's not a Hasidic Jew. And to avoid getting labeled as a bear by gay men.

1. The Magnum

2. The Unfortunate Ginger

3. The Victorian Strongman

4. The Misguided Dictator

5. The Thompson and Thomson

6. The Waters

7. The Hulkamaniac

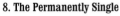

8. The Permanently Single

9. The Thatch

10. The Too Much Time
On His Hands

FASHION DESIGNER

"If you aren't part of the now, then you're part of the not now—and that doesn't mean the future, as the future starts now, not yesterday, and you can't be there tomorrow if you're not here now."

That is the most profound statement I have ever made, and one that I totally live my life by. As a fashion designer, I need to be NOW, or tomorrow I'll be nothing. And fashion is not nothing, it is everything.

People who don't care about looking cool actually repulse me. People who watch television and only go to exhibitions if they're free actually are the scourge of the Earth. I'm a free thinker and I express myself through the medium of clothing. Layering fabric, contrasting textures, experimenting with millinary, and accessorizing with found items is how I furnish my existence.

Since I made my "NOW STATEMENT," or the NS as me and my close circle of like-minded friends call it, I have lessened my vocal output. Speaking takes me away from the moment, from the now. I'm a nucleus in a powerful cell, a forward-thinking proton. My visions are lithium, my tears of passion make them explode into life.

At present, I am wearing an overcoat made from turf. I cut the panels like I would cloth and stitched them together using gardening twine. When I'm not wearing it I hose it down to keep it green. There is so much scope for eco-clothing, but I think I have taken this concept as far as it will go. I apply fertilizer on the shoulders to give me tufted epaulets. Grass is ecology's army, soldiers stand to attention across the globe, and that's what I'm representing with the military-inspired tailoring. When I take the coat off, my clothes are covered in mud, it's disgusting but I am using the stained garments in my new collection. I am going to try and work out a way of covering them in slogans grown out of moss.

I design couture solely for myself; I am the only one capable of doing my designs justice. For everyone else there are t-shirts. The designs for these vary—at the moment I am in to batik and studs. Think Indonesian tribes playing cover versions of The Ramones; Sumatra vs Sid Vicious; a durian fruit poking through a thin sheet of butter-soft lambskin leather; hot java coffee thrown over the torso of a man in a gimp mask.

There's been a lot of discourse that the t-shirts are $150; people seem to think that it's too much money. People are idiots. Considering the customer is getting to fully immerse themselves in the now and live and breathe the NS statement, I think it's a steal. Anyone who doubts me and my vision doesn't deserve to have my name rubbing against their nape.

GRAPHIC DESIGNER.

Ask a hipster what his job is and the chances are his answer will be, "Graphic designer, obvs."

Your next question should always be, "Are you working at the moment?" He'll probably say no—after all, it's a well-known fact that eight out of ten unemployed hipsters are graphic designers. The remaining two are either in bands or attempting to manage one.

Graphic designers are easily spotted. They will look like all the others, with their thick-rimmed glasses and smart shirts. They carry their MacBooks with them in vintage leather satchels, plus a Moleskin notebook for sketching fonts. They loiter in niche galleries and moonlight as graffiti artists. If they're wearing chinos, they'll also be wearing expensive brogues. If they're wearing jeans, they'll be wearing an enormous pair of Nikes and flipping up the peak of their limited-edition cap to complete the look.

Despite sneering at mainstream culture, they desire to work at a large advertising agency. Look through their outbox and you'll find secret emails to Leo Burnett, AKQA, Pentagram, and Iris, begging for some feedback on their portfolio, pleading for a job or even an unpaid work placement. But on the surface, they're happy being part of a design "collective."

What this usually means is that they have other unemployed friends who enjoy messing about on Photoshop and can spend hours debating the superiority of Wim Crouwel's Gridnik over Adrian Frutiger's Avenir, or discussing Eric Gill's relationships with his daughter and his dog. They look down on those who say, "I like that font." It's not a font, it's a typeface.

They yearn to live in Berlin. They romanticize the city, dreaming of walking under its imposing architecture and showing off their Russian-prison-inspired tattoos as they swim in the Bauhaus-designed Stadtbad Mitte. They long to start a new life in a Friedrichshain squat, fall in love with a German skinhead, snort their weight in cheap speed, chain-smoke and stare at the frozen Spree, compete in the annual Hipster Olympics, and learn German by immersing themselves in the anarchic creative underground.

Sadly, funding this dream is expensive, so as long as they're designing album covers for unsigned punk bands, spending hours on pitches they will never win, coming up with logos for sneaker boutiques that never open, and drinking locally brewed ale in nameless bars, the German capital will never be anything more than a utopia they read about on their favorite websites: Slow Travel Berlin, Lodown, and KultMucke. Their emptiness is compounded by the knowledge that they'll never go on a walk of the city with other Instagrammers, and never know if St. Agnes looks better when given a blanket of Walden or Sutro.

GOTH LOLITA

Korea didn't smile much. It wasn't because she had bad teeth, far from it.

Her parents invested thousands in the best orthodontist money could buy. Mummy and Daddy, who still lived comfortably in a detached barn conversion just outside Guildford, had no idea their daughter's symmetrical grin was so rarely revealed. Speaking on the phone, she sounded as middle class and enthusiastic as when they had dropped her off at her new university lodgings just months ago. Mr and Mrs Brown also had no idea that their only child, Sarah, was now going by the name of Korea, and running a monthly electro night called "Communist Party," where she did a performance art piece under the moniker of Kim Jong Skillz.

Korea was a diminutive 5 ft 2 in, with dark almond-shaped eyes. Her hair, naturally mousy, was cut into a severe chin-length bob, and dyed the same static black as a witch's wig at Halloween. Unusually for a girl from Surrey, a girl who had grown up playing hockey and was captain of the Lacrosse team, her skin always had a deathly pallor; now it looked almost ecru in some lights.

But the most noticeable thing about Korea was not her half crescent eyes that hissed a vicious scrawl of black liquid liner, or her bizarre Lolita-style outfit she had purchased from a sex

stall at Camden Market, but her lips, which she held in a pouty and permanent scowl.

The mouth that she insisted on keeping closed, the one that held two rows of gleaming white teeth, was decorated with a greasy layer of boot polish. She preferred the type that came in a tin—it was cheap and easy to apply with a lip brush. Plus, it had better staying power than lipstick and, she was sure, held some sort of conditioning treatment, too. "It makes shoes supple, so why not my mouth?" she had once posted on her tumblr.

It was ironic that she even cared, considering she was regarded by most as being almost mute. The mouth, always covered in boot polish, always in that downward pout, was rarely used. She had plenty to say, but she had even more to keep secret.

Upon arriving at university, Sarah had decided to embrace being away from the gaze of her well-meaning but stifling parents and bleach her hair. Using some of her new riches (student bank account overdraft), she had bought a canister of Clairol dye and set about giving herself a sexy makeover.

But, as with most DIY beauty treatments, it went horribly wrong, leaving her with a nest of orangey rat tails, split ends, and bright yellow roots. Devastated, she decided to hide the damage and dye black what was left of her long hair, hacking off the ends to hide the damage.

It was a few days later that she was mistaken for a Korean exchange student and the charade officially began. She had been looking at books for her history of art course when the handsome stranger—he was tall and thin as a rake, wearing women's jeans and a checked shirt—had approached her. They made small talk, her mumbling through pursed lips, implying that she was an exotic exchange student who could barely speak English.

And now here she was propping up the bar at her club night, drinking a warm bottle of beer through a straw. Too afraid to open her pretty mouth and lose everything.

FASHION MODEL

Statistics reveal that the weight of a typical model today is ⅟₂₃ that of the average woman.

It's a figure that Annaleise Prost is perfectly happy with... in more ways than one. The model almost breaks out into a wry smile as she recites her typical daily meal plan. "Black coffee, five Skittles, and chocolax." But chocolate-flavored laxatives aren't the only way she satisfies her sweet tooth.

"If I'm on my way to a shoot," she says, staring at the ceiling and elongating her hollow face. "I'll, like, take a bite from one of those fun-sized Snickers bars then throw it out of the car window. I'm just like other any healthy girl in her twenties."

Annaleise, whose 30AA – 23 – 29 figure has made her the go-to clothes horse for some of the world's biggest designers and the darling of the London fashion scene, is dismissive of her success.

"I just find it all so boring," she sighs. With her shaved eyebrows, crewcut, and septum piercing, she is more squatter than society girl—which is probably a source of surprise for her ex-classmates from the well-to-do Cheltenham Ladies College.

Her arms, long and sinewy, hang lifelessly by her side as she turns to the cameras, expressionless. Her thighs, concave and threadlike, boast a covetable "double fist" gap at the top. Photographers commend her ability to look entirely vacant, her immunity to joy. Fashion designers love her figure, with curves so easy to dress. Editors adore her spunk and attitude.

She likes her large blue eyes, which are framed by translucent lashes and possess a spooky watery quality. They are the only color on her since she had the whole of her left arm tattooed black.

"I had a sleeve before, it had koi carp and two geishas throttling each other, but I got bored of fish and pale women so I just had it all filled in.

"A friend of mine is an artist and he's making some sketches for a new design that I plan to place on top of the current one. It is going to look like a monkey has scrawled obscenities on a chalkboard. It's playing on the idea of apes writing Shakespeare. I'll use lazer removal to burn the designs onto my skin."

Ask Annaleise any question and her answer will be the same: boring, bored, boredom. Making thousands for wearing expensive clothes, living in a warehouse in Hackney Downs, dating Hollywood actors... it's all such a drag.

Does anything make her happy?

"No."

SOCIAL MEDIA GUY

They didn't call him Rainman because he looked like Dustin Hoffman.

Nor was it anything to do with him being good at gambling, or even being on the autism spectrum (although his ex-girlfriend suspected he was). They called him Rainman because he wore a pair of gum boots every day. "Fuck off," he'd guffaw. "They're not gum boots, they're Hunter boots, they're DESIGNER!"

DESIGNER, always spoken as if it was being sounded out to a far-away foreigner, was Rainman's favorite word; he loved it. He loved it as much as he loved his job, he loved it as much as he loved all the money his job had made him and all the DESIGNER clothes (and gum boots) he owned. He loved being an Independent Social Marketing Consultant. If it was on trend, he would have liked to ditch the boots and wear a pair of black and white spatz with his skin-tight jeans (Levis, not DESIGNER, still cool) and his oversized cable-knit cardigan (cashmere, obviously DESIGNER, and it had cost him a LOT).

In this parallel universe, he'd resemble a clean-shaven cad that had been spat out from a 1920s prohibition speakeasy straight into present day Shoreditch. His hair would be the same, a greaser quiff, and he'd still have good skin thanks to moisturizing twice a day with Clinique products. He'd be taller than 5 ft 7 in, as the spats could have secret lifts built in like the shoes Tom Cruise is rumored to wear. He'd have some metal panels on the toes, too, giving him some "tap dance vibes." Then he could tell people he literally made his money "pay per click." What a sense of humor!

Wherever he went, Rainman carried all the latest Apple products: iPhone, MacBook, iPad, and iPod. He didn't need them all, but they were expensive and made him look "swag." He had a selection of matching cases for them, some Louis Vuitton, some Mulberry—all very very DESIGNER. He had others too, rare ones made from animal pelts, and some made from panties from a Tokyo vending machine—but they were for home use only.

"Technology is what separates us from apes," Rainman mumbled through a mouthful of lamb doner kebab. "Did you know I ordered this kebab using an app on my iPhone?"

New Capital Kebab was deserted apart from the two of them. His date looked wearily at the behemoth chunk of lamb that slowly sweated juice from every scar. From where she sat, the meat seemed to hold a caring gaze over the glass hot counters and their fried-chicken prisoners. "Kind of like a nurse with some premature babies," she mused.

Her eyes rolled as Rainman described helping a shoe label increase its Twitter followers by 80 per cent. She tried to look interested in what he was saying, forcing herself to listen. "For fuck's sake," she thought, "please just shut up about fucking Twitter."

Looking at Rainman she tried to work out if he had large thumbs from all the tweeting. She ended up glancing at the sauce that had oozed out from the end of his pita straight onto the screen of the iPad. She wished that he'd see and go nuts, maybe he'd accidentally drop it and crack the screen. If he made a scene she could run off. Anything was better than this.

TRUST FUND ARTIST

Being an artist is hard work.

People say, "It's not a real job," and they're right, it isn't, it's a calling. I've always said I have paint instead of blood, and that's why I spend my day hunched over an easel and not some yellowing PC in a drab office. Actually, I've never even worked in an office, it's beneath me. And I only use Macs. I live only to create.

My life is hard, really hard. I live in my studio, it's in the Meatpacking District on 15th Street. My parents bought it for me, but it's not as if I'm some spoiled brat, it's because they believe in my gift and it's an investment for my future.

Mom came to see me yesterday after she'd been playing paddle tennis at the New York Athletics Club with my aunt. She didn't stay long, she was pissed that all the coffee mugs she bought me from Saks Fifth Avenue were full of cigarette butts. I was like, "Sorry Mom, but I'm exploring the existentialism of blank space, can you just leave?"

I have a trust fund, but that doesn't mean I'm not part of the struggle. It's not as if I just have millions of dollars in the bank. My parents' estate assigns me just ten grand a month, and with that I have to buy materials, get food, and fund my social life. I rarely have more than ten bucks by the fifteenth. It's hard.

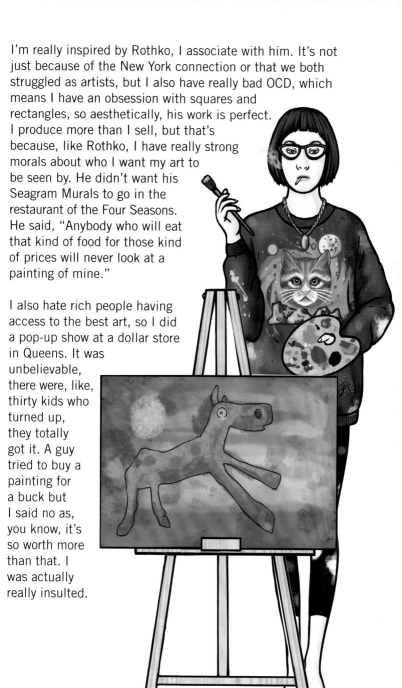

I'm really inspired by Rothko, I associate with him. It's not just because of the New York connection or that we both struggled as artists, but I also have really bad OCD, which means I have an obsession with squares and rectangles, so aesthetically, his work is perfect. I produce more than I sell, but that's because, like Rothko, I have really strong morals about who I want my art to be seen by. He didn't want his Seagram Murals to go in the restaurant of the Four Seasons. He said, "Anybody who will eat that kind of food for those kind of prices will never look at a painting of mine."

I also hate rich people having access to the best art, so I did a pop-up show at a dollar store in Queens. It was unbelievable, there were, like, thirty kids who turned up, they totally got it. A guy tried to buy a painting for a buck but I said no as, you know, it's so worth more than that. I was actually really insulted.

VINTAGE STORE WORKER

Steve looked like a frog. That was why he decided to "get a haircut."

Not only did his over-styled thatch—like a rat's nest on top with two gelled sections flanking his face—detract attention from his bug eyes and crooked teeth, it also made women want to sleep with him, a novelty that he was sure would never wear off.

It was 2002, and The Strokes were the coolest band in the world. Suddenly, it was more desirable than ever to be a rockstar and Steve wanted a part of that. It didn't matter that he was as apt a musician as he was a looker, the three chords he could strangle out of his guitar were all that it took to land him in a band with four other guys from his hometown.

As the popularity of The Carrier Bags increased, so did the ferocity of his hair. He wore sunglasses all year round. He looked like a chump, but teenage girls are fools and willingly fell into bed with him. Soon, he felt as if he had shagged every woman in his dead-end provincial town, and decided that he had no choice but to move to the big city.

The sirens startled him to start with, and as he made his way tentatively through Camden on his first Friday night in London, he noticed that his hair wasn't the biggest, nor were his jeans the skinniest in this part of town. It was a matter of weeks before he realized no one was interested in his band, and the women—loud, brash, and thinner than him—preferred cocaine to cock. Well, at least HIS cock, he rued.

Life was miserable, and to add insult to injury he was forced to work in a vintage store. Each day, as he folded musty pairs of Levis and neatened row upon row of moth-eaten Hawaiian shirts, he muttered to himself, indignantly. The only plus side was that his measly pay wasn't enough to cover both his grotty room in Willesden and food, so his legs were skinnier than ever.

Ten years on, and he's still selling second-hand sunglasses, battered sneakers, and threadbare t-shirts. He's almost thirty-five and, despite a rapidly receding hairline, he still continues to backcomb and gel what's left of his crowning glory. He thinks it makes it look thicker. It doesn't. Steve is still living in squalor. He is still making music that nobody will ever want to listen to. No one wants to sleep with him. Steve is still ugly. He has nothing.

BAND MANAGER

Cynical people are scornful of those who manage bands... with good reason.

The really fun part of meeting one, other than feeding them earnest (and often cruelly false) feedback on their charge's latest EP, comes later. That's the point when you can dissect your conversation and work out what path led the misguided fool to the wholly thankless job of managing a group of youngsters who are deluded enough to believe you can make a living out of playing an instrument while smoking a cigarette.

If the band is famous, then they've lucked out. If the band is unsigned, then they'll fall into one of three main categories. If they are related to someone in the band then they're doing it out of duty. If not, either they are totally untalented and desperate to somehow get a chance to feed at the fame trough, or they used to be in a band and never made it past the spending-all-their-money-on-rehearsing-three-nights-a-week stage. Whatever their reason, it's likely they're gonna be a dickhead.

Ask a band manager what he does, and he'll make out he's the backbone of the group. He's Brian Epstein, he's Colonel Tom Parker, he's Malcom McClaren. Secretly, his hero is Tony Defries, David Bowie's one-time manager who earned more than The Thin White Duke did.

Their duties are many: call record labels, beg someone at record label to listen to a demo/see a show, call back record label and make idle threats about missing a "once in a generation chance," call band, make sure band know to go to the studio or venue, call uninterested journalists, lobby frazzled editors who are more worried about flat plans than Clapton's answer to Iggy Pop, get gigs for the band, buy guitar strings for the bassist as he's tired, call the dealer… It doesn't take long to do these things, but they'll emphatically state it's a 24/7 lifestyle.

Despite being so busy championing art, most of the time they'll hold down a job somewhere else. After all, even the manager of "the next XX" has bills to pay. Usually the job will be office-based, allowing the "manager" to make the most of a franking machine (handy for sending demos) and a desk complete with phone and internet access for those all-important managerial calls and emails.

Financial reward is rare, or a pittance, so what's in it for them? A hefty slice of the action. Invites, meeting "cool people," parties, festivals, late nights, women, the post-show rider, lines, joints… and the opportunity to play God. "No one's coming to the shows, we need a gimmick. Look in that bag, there are some accessories, get 'em on and get on stage. There might be a guy from *Stool Pigeon* magazine here tonight."

HIPSTER DOGS

Hipsters love dogs. But only ones who have been so inbred that their eyes bulge from their heads, they have trouble breathing, and are small enough to be transported in a Fjällräven Kanken backpack.

In the past, man relied upon a dog to guard his sheep and family from predators. Today's modern, "creative" man needs a dog to guard his latte while he reboots the router in his open-plan office, or to attract simpering women as he queues up for an overpriced pulled-pork sandwich from a brightly colored food truck.

It's crucial that these moustache twiddlers and Zooey Deschanel wannabes have a "cool dog." One that they can carry under one arm like a newspaper when meeting friends for an organic coffee or a craft beer, or one that fits neatly into a wicker basket or backpack when cycling to pick up the latest issue of *AnOtherMan* or a batch of organic crumpets.

For this reason, they are most likely to be seen doting on a Bichon Frise, French Bulldog, Boston Terrier, Pug, or Dachshund. They love these cute breeds that look good in little coats or fancy dress costumes and can be easily adorned with accessories that take attention away from their snoring, labored breathing patterns, and exaggerated traits.

They feel confident taking their little canine friends to the local bar, where they know they can order a homemade dog biscuit at the same time as asking for a bloody mary and a bag of hand-fried, gluten-free pretzels. They remain oblivious as drunk people almost tread on the poor mites, who are forced to cower between their owner's own unsteady legs.

All these adventures—and the fuss and "awwws"—mean that many of these dogs get their own Twitter account or blog. Surely you must know that the dog has a really valid opinion? Especially with such an empowering name as Sam/Jamie/Henry/Maxine/Daisy/Timmy… "Can't wait to get my paws on the new iPhone," and "Just barked at a bench. It's a post-modern phenomenon #YOLO," are typical doggie shares. Hipster dog owners really are hilarious.

The recent invention of meat-free dog food such as V-Dog (yes, really) means that now vegans can join in the fun and games of dog ownership. God bless those lethargic and anaemic hounds, forced to live a lifestyle that goes against thousands of years of evolution—usually while being made to balance a pair of thick-rimmed spectacles on their snout. To cap it all, in August 2011, the cool dogs of Brooklyn were invited to perform at the Hipster Dog Pageant—the judges were looking for "the most ironic and indifferent dog." Urgh.

ROCKABILLIES

Hey baby, looking at the past like it was better than now is such a gas, ain't it?

People seem to find it impossible to develop their own sense of self, preferring to rape the past for ideas on how to dress, what to listen to, and even what slang to use.

At the extreme end of the spectrum, Rockabillies are guilty of swapping their rose-tinted glasses for periscopal ones that are aimed firmly in the direction of 60 years ago. They embrace a certain lifestyle, yearning for the days when they could only watch black and white TV for a few hours a day, not be able to buy pasta from the supermarket, and never have to turn on the radio and hear a Rihanna song. The good old days, when women were expected to use a broom to beat rugs outside the front of the house in full view of the neighbors, black people were rarely seen and never heard (apart from their records, which were OK to like), and anyone who wore a red shirt was accused of being a communist. Halcyon times, indeed.

The ideas of a Rockabilly teeter on the edge of the bizarre but, on the whole, they look great. So, it's no surprise that hipsters, perhaps inspired by the xenomorphs made popular in the Alien franchise, have begun brazenly stealing their style.

For guys, greaser quiffs, well-worn leather jackets, stone-washed Levi's with turn-ups, shiny boots, white vests, and red braces are becoming wardrobe staples. Girls are cutting their fringes to an inch beneath their hairline and wearing cat-eye spectacles or, even worse, getting involved with burlesque. All these things look great with a pin-up tattoo/moustache/pug/retro accessory.

Of course, the nu-Rockabilly will name drop bands and anachronistic "50s things" to make it look like they're part of the lifestyle and not just a poser. "I love The Cramps, and milkshakes," they'll muse, hoping the person they're speaking to doesn't remember they're supposed to be a vegan.

Rockabillies prefer to socialize en masse. They call people "Daddio" and "Square." They idolize Fonzie from *Happy Days*, refusing to admit they're more of a Richie Cunningham and at school got laid less than Potsie.

They also live in fear of their past—avoiding the bars and clubs they frequented two years ago when they listened to dubstep, or six years ago when it was cool to like bands beginning with "The," in case they meet an old acquaintance capable of questioning their retro credentials.

Do you think they would abandon their love affair with neckerchiefs and brothel creepers if they knew the world's most successful rockabilly is awful Eighties pop star Shakin' Stevens?

RAVE PROMOTER

Just like doctors and their Hippocratic Oath, those who put on warehouse parties claim to be governed by the same ideals: to ride the crest of a cultural wave and simultaneously be a catalyst for an as-yet-unknown artistic movement that will change society.

When rave culture first began to take shape in the late 1980s, it was a simple premise. A thousand people turned up in a random field to take drugs and dance until dawn, while the police and an angry farmer looked on, their expressions morphing from bemused to irate and back again.

However, a modern day rave is a chance for hipsters to show off how many drugs they can take, to wear ridiculously unsuitable clothes, and tantalize their senses with a lazer show and smoke machine—not to mention take photos of each other wearing Raybans and showing off some serious side-boob.

For the most part, the people who attend these events, held anywhere from an underground car park to an abandoned old-folks home, are not music lovers but scene junkies. Often there is more culture in a pot of yogurt than at one of these shindigs, where a straw poll of future ambitions will reveal the most popular aspiration is to be one of the glass-eyed sluts in an American Apparel advert.

In a bid to seem more edgy, and perhaps to divert attention away from the fact that you've just paid an extortionate amount to dance in a car park where there's a real risk of breaking your ankle on a stray supermarket plastic bag, promoters often throw in a few sexy extras to the night's proceedings. Strippers, dance troupes, and performance artists share the bill with DJs who have limited ability and stupid names, and bands who play heavy metal cover versions of old Sega 8-bit themes.

The posters are painstakingly created on Photoshop, but arrive at the party and you'll be greeted with banners that look like they've been painted by a team of nursery school children off their little heads on Neon Nerds and Sherbert Dib Dabs. This is especially true of parties with a theme—Street Fighter 2 Turbo Smash Bash; Home and Garden Décor to Rakecore; Wardrobe Malfunction: Punishment of the Fashion Weak; Cereal Killers vs Crunchy Nutters.

You don't need to be a mind reader to work out that as far as the promoter's concerned, he's a Tweeting hybrid of Andy Warhol and Jesus. But, with his oversized glasses, pick of the girls, cringe-worthy musical aspirations, and scraggly mullet, he's more like David Koresh.

SKATEBOARDER

Hobbies we have as children are usually left behind once we hit adolescence.

Playing with My Little Ponies, collecting dolls, running around with a gun made from a stick, or dressing like a cowboy for a trip to the supermarket are all foibles of youth that do not translate well to the adult world.

Of course, some people continue their childhood activities well into adulthood. The girl who doted on her Tiny Tears might now have a spare bedroom full of creepily realistic Reborn Dolls. The boy who dressed as a cowboy is quite possibly a key member of a historical re-enactment group or just a local lunatic you know not to make eye-contact with. Childhood hobbies rarely translate into the behavior of a well-rounded adult.

However, a forty year old on a skateboard is regarded as ok and, sometimes, even cool. But, let's be honest—it's a bit sad to see a grown man wearing a pair of Dickies jeans and a Vans hoodie skateboarding to work. It is even worse to see a man approaching middle age picking up his kids from school decked out in a New Era fitted cap and Supra Skytops. It's pretty embarrassing to see a grown man dressing in the same brands as his teenage son, but unfortunately it's not that uncommon as the love of trucks, decks, and wheels is passed on from generation to generation. Witnessing a man with graying stubble, who is dressed like a member of the 80s thrash metal band he used to listen to during high school, kick-flipping to a chorus of cheers from a gang of 11-year-olds cocooned in helmets and knee pads sitting on the wall of a public skatepark rarely raises eyebrows.

Like someone who has suffered an extreme trauma, the mindset of an adult skateboarder is usually fixed at a certain point in time. A time when he wanted to "fight the man," listened to Rage Against The Machine really loud on his walkman, moaned that the local council had made the streets in their town center cobbled, and generally smelt quite bad. Old habits die hard—they are still partial to drinking cheap booze on street corners, wear a dislocated wrist as a badge of pride, quote lines from Harmony Korine's cult movie Kids, and carry a skate tool in their back pocket.

These days, older skateboarders like to make extended videos of them and their friends doing tricks and having gnarly fun at different locales using the hi-tech gadgets their well-paid jobs (usually in graphic design or PR) have brought them. They spend hours hunched over their Macs carefully editing the footage, giving it a Flying Lotus soundtrack and a bleached effect. Then, as they upload it to Vimeo, they stand defiant and flushed with pride that the allegiance they pledged to the "sport" when they were seven years old still stands true.

STREETWEAR FIEND

A trip to Japan can mean a chance to spend the night in a hotel where you sleep on your back in a sort of coffin-meets-desk drawer.

Or it could mean the chance to immerse yourself in a culture so different to your own that you feel like you've landed on a foreign planet. New cuisine, enormous sky scrapers, toilets that clean your ass and dry it at the press of a button, thousands of years' worth of history—and some questionable animated porn—await you in the Land of the Rising Sun.

But, to the hipster tracksuit tourist, the only thing worth seeing is some seriously rare streetwear. He's the kind of guy who checks Hypebeast as soon as he wakes up, and treats High Snobriety as his newspaper. He owns two of everything—one to wear, one to keep "fresh" and stored away neatly in a drawer in his bedroom.

Back home, he didn't have to think twice about parting with hundreds of dollars for a SASQUATCHfabrix t-shirt. He only wears 45rpm jeans, and today's he's wearing his favorite Visvim FB Waxed 2-Tone kicks. People at home teased him, said they were "Fugly," but they said that about his Nike x Supreme creps too. They clearly know jack shit. They cost him nearly a grand on eBay. They're that cool.

His eyes glaze over as he walks past the BAPE megastore in Shibuya. He has to pause, suddenly the top-fastened collar of his chambray shirt feels very tight. He's worried that there will be a large sweat patch forming on the small of his back as he adjusts his Mastertex-04 backpack over his Sacai gilet.

Inside, he can't help but gently touch every item on display. He picks up a 12,000 yen Kaws vs BAPE t-shirt to admire the print. The guy behind the counter looks up from his iPad, pissed off that he'll have to actually do some work and refold the tee. Streetwear boy is undeterred. The spring of the hoodies make him shake his head in a sort of lusty disbelief. His collar's getting tight again. OMG, limited edition G-Shock watches!

He made the journey to Tokyo alone, to him it's equal to a pilgrimage, a time for reflection and questions. Besides, his girlfriend would be horrified if she knew how much money he had already spent on this trip, and planned to spend in this shop within the next hour.

Hipsters like having things that no one else has, which is why limited edition streetwear is so appealing. It's comfortable yet stylish, the Stussy store plays cool music, and being ahead of the pack means shopping trips to the Far East. What's not to like?

SNEAKER HEAD

Carefully raising the lid of the box, his face twists and convulses.

In the shadow of his bedroom, he mutates from Sméagol to Gollum as he realizes he is now in possession of an extremely rare pair of Nikes. His eyes, glowing with lust, barely move from the nylon and leather monstrosities before him. "The Speed Art Spongebob Squarepants Nike Dunks are finally in my possession!" he mutters. Gingerly, he strokes the stitching, and lifts one from its branded tissue paper so he can examine the sole. "Perfect," he squeals, quickly forgetting that these just set him back hundreds of dollars.

He quickly takes some photographs of them ready to post to the internet, before putting the box safely back into its cardboard sarcophagus and stacking it neatly on top of several other pristine boxes—some of which date all the way back to 1992. Welcome to the seedy world of the sneaker aficionado.

Oblivious to the sad fact that there are millions of people across the world who can't afford shoes, he pays huge amounts of money for shoes produced for a pittance in sweatshops with the single aim of keeping them in a box away from view—and feet.

Trying to decipher the crowing soliloquys of sneaker freaks in forum posts titled "fresh treds," "deadstock Adidas ObyO," and "unworn Nike Air CB34 from 1995" is similar to how the police force of Victorian England must have felt when eavesdropping on Cockneys talking about "apples and pears" or "oats and chaff."

The world of a sneaker collector is one of avarice and one-upmanship. They look through websites such as Sneakerpedia as if it was a bingo card, ticking off the styles they own—or used to own but have since sold on. Collecting is an expensive hobby with some rare models going for over $1,000 on eBay. And their value doesn't necessarily diminish even if they have been cut up and used to make a new "customized" version by one of the scene's many admired reworkers. These remodeled treds are popular with streetwear fashionistas and low-end rappers, who might ask for their name and a sketch of their gold teeth to be garishly painted on the Frankenshoe.

These collectors paw Sneaker Freaker magazine like a rat shown a catalog of cheese, grabbing at the shoes they wish they had in the footwear mausoleum that is slowly building at the back of their wardrobe. "They're important cultural artefacts," they say, trying hard to sound earnest.

Some of the most desired "kicks" are ones that are the result of collaborations between sports brands and designers, streetwear labels, boutique sneaker stores, or artists. The Jeremy Scott for Adidas trainers that featured cuddly pandas on the tongues or wings on the sides, are unsightly but lusted after. Crossovers between Adidas and Japanese brand BAPE don't look particularly special but change hands for hundreds. Similarly, the Nike x Supreme line looks like hiking shoes you wouldn't want to be seen dead in—perhaps why the majority of them have remained in the box.

no.# 20

HEADDRESS IDIOT

At some point in the last ten years, music festivals metamorphosed from being a place to drink warm, overpriced beer and watch bands, to being a catwalk for dickheads of all shapes and sizes—on and off stage.

With every weekend of the Summer now crammed with at least three different events—from one-day folk fests in the countryside to three-day drug and dubstep binges in a disused warehouse, it's proving hard to separate the wheat from the chaff—is everyone at these things a twat?

When immersed in a sea of festival dickheads; when you think your eyes are going to bleed from witnessing tide upon tide of fancy dress mishaps; when your ears are ringing from the sub-standard soundsystems overlaid with screeching pill-heads calling out that year's festival meme of choice and you think if you ever see another falafel stall again it'll be too soon, remember this: the skinny obnoxious dude in the Native American headdress is King Cock.

He's impossible to miss. He's the one dressed like a member of the Village People in a huge feathered war bonnet, with red, white, and black feathers framing his face and falling all the way to near his elbows. He could be eighteen and the hottest guy in high school, or he could be the grizzly faced, pickled-liver account manager from a big name design agency whose wife is pissed off he's left her at home with the baby while he stuffs his nasal cavities with their vacation fund. But what unites them is their longing to be the center of attention.

They know—regardless of weather—that the headdress requires being as near-naked as possible. Their girlfriend, or festival hook-up, is inevitably the one who has brought enough neon paint to cover a bus.

Look at how he's smeared in paint! Look at the way the handprints glide down his glorious, hairless torso! Look at how his plastic Wayfarers give him an "I don't give a fuck!" edge. His jeans are so low on the hips you can see his pants! What a hero.

He almost hopes it'll rain, as it'll provide an excuse for him to get his "proper festival gear" on— a Barbour waxed jacket and a pair of Hunter boots.

As the day progresses, Headdress Idiot will start to believe more and more that he is Jim Morrison. He'll elbow you in the face as he positions himself, Christ-like with his arms outstretched, in the busiest part of the crowd, not caring that he is blocking people's views with his stupid hat.

With his tatty beer cup in his hand, he tries to pout like The Doors' iconic frontman, but actually ends up drooling all over himself. By now, his neon body paint, once so vibrant and expertly applied, has become a smeared mess. Like a pizza manhandled in its box and splattered all over the lid.

These are the pictures he'll detag on Facebook when back at work on Monday.

DRUG DEALER

It's an easy trap to fall in to, but remember, your drug dealer is not your friend. Many hipsters aren't quite able to get their head around that, and are often left doubly out of pocket when they end up buying their local pusher's drinks for them all night long.

It must be testimony to the caliber of drugs they're getting hooked up with that many hipsters are unable to see that there is some sort of ruse going on—that man who is being given wads of crumpled up bank notes is simultaneously moaning that he's utterly broke. "Shout us a beer?" he'll whine. If you have any sense, your reply will be, "No!"

And don't listen to any chat about "overheads"—he's selling low-grade narcotics, not managing an office block.

If you are on good enough terms to ask the guy to bring some supplies to your home, he's going to expect something to drink and the chances are he'll also ask for something to snack on. In their mind, they give and therefore have the right to also take—and that includes Oreos and Doritos.

Selling drugs can be a competitive business, so dealers will go all out to give themselves the edge. If they're using themselves, then it's unlikely that their USP will be fantastic customer service—unless you put an order in five hours earlier than you actually want to pick up. It's more likely there will be some sort of bespoke packaging involved. Perhaps a wrap made from the personal ads found in the back of a porn mag, or maybe an unusual Stars and Stripes baggy. They're not stupid—they know that if they give you your five Ritalin in a chichi package you're going to be a flash prick and will Instagram the hell out of it. The result: more flash pricks will want some pills delivered in a magic bag and soon you'll be getting new, equally clueless clients... #businessplan.

They're all about aesthetics, despite mouthfuls of browning teeth (thanks to a nasty little speed habit). From their snazzy clothing—which takes inspiration from Paulie from the Sopranos and Ray Liotta in Goodfellas—to selling ketamine that has been gently scented with vanilla or sandalwood, the hipster drug dealer makes up for his sketchiness with his attention to detail.

And, just like his clients, he has ideas above his station, which is why he will introduce you to investors and business partners—basically bywords for people who have lent him money to pick up some product—and are now hanging around to make sure they get that money back. Be careful, they'll want drinks and snacks, too.

BARISTA

That man who just served you a coffee isn't a barista, he's actually a photographer, writer, singer, designer, artist—basically anything other than "man who makes coffee."

Couldn't you tell by the poetry tattooed across his hands and the gentle curve of his eyebrows that he is more than just a man who serves you hot drinks? And what about her, in her original 1950s cat-eye spectacles and one-inch long fringe? Didn't you recognize her from the feminist poetry slam last week?

On the whole, the people asking you if you want cream on that hot chocolate are moralistic creatives, doing their best to keep their heads above water in an unforgiving capitalist society. That's why they work part-time at a non-chain coffee shop that only sells organic and Fair Trade products. Duh.

But that doesn't mean they don't take their jobs very, very seriously. These cool cat coffee jockeys rarely smile—there's no joking about perfectly roasted beans. They're the first to point out that "it's not a cookie, it's a biscotti," and when they ask you if you want a "grande or venti" sized beverage, that's their Italian night-school class being put to good use.

If you do end up in conversation, you'll discover that misery truly loves company. They'll explain they're really a writer or photographer, and they're successful but only ever get unpaid work, so have to also work behind this very counter serving people just like you in order to fund their art.

They might reveal whimsical fantasies of persuading the store manager to allow them to do an exhibition of some of their photography in this very locale. They think their adventurous snaps of a band you've never heard of before would look "absolutely stunning" against the exposed brick walls. If they find out you could help them on their journey, they'll sweeten you with an extra shot of coffee, or take that extra bit longer to ensure your milk is well frothed. They're good at that, they've been doing it a while now.

In areas like New York's Brooklyn, Chicago's Wicker Park, Sydney's New Town, and London's Dalston, coffee shops are seemingly popping up overnight, meaning people yet to accept that their blog or handmade jewelry line isn't their shortcut to fame and fortune can make just enough money to pay their share of rent in the warehouse space they live in with twelve others. And at the end of the working day, they get to take the stale biscotti and muffins home, too. This is nothing to be sniffed at when their degree in Fine Art has left them thirty years old, depressed, and barely earning the minimum wage to pay the line rental on their iPhone.

BURLESQUE DANCER

"What first attracted me to the art form of burlesque was the feminist aspect of it," she'll say, applying another coating of Besame lipstick.

"This," she'll explain, pointing at the golden bullet, "is the same color and brand as Marilyn Monroe wore."

The burlesque dancer will turn and pout in the mirror. In the reflection a tube of Pringles and an iPhone are clearly visible behind her. "I like to live the 1940s lifestyle as authentically as possible. This is my art, I live it, breathe it, sleep it, eat it," she'll say before quickly shimmying her shoulders up and down and making her way to the stage door.

Many women have fallen under the spell of burlesque, a form of erotic entertainment where silver poles and g-strings are replaced by titillation and coquettish teasing. Girls of all shapes and sizes pretend to be Dita Von Teese as they strut around on stage wearing waist-high knickers and sequinned pasties over their nipples. They trowel on make-up to drag-queen standards and style their hair into finger curls, both lengthy and somewhat tiresome processes.

People can be scornful of burlesque and those hipsters who admire it. "They just do it because they're too fat to work at Spearmint Rhino," men will sneer, while some women label the performers "vile attention seekers." The dreadful Cher and Christina Aguilera movie, Burlesque, has done little to make it a credible art form.

While burlesque once was as funny, sexy, clever, and daring as its advocates say, these days it has been subjected to a stream of newcomers who think that anyone can do it, which has somewhat diluted the "art form." A real-life equivalent would be making Bucks Fizz from Lambrini and orange cordial, instead of Champagne and freshly squeezed orange juice.

For some bizarre reason, hoards of women think that all they have to do to reinvent themselves as modern day pin-ups is to put on a corset and some long gloves and take to a dimly-lit stage, slowly stroking their chest by starting at the finger-tips of the opposite arm, or turning around and giving an exaggerated wink to an embarrassed crowd. They give themselves ridiculous monikers like "Penny Drops" or "Cookie Crumbles," and spend small fortunes on handmade lingerie in bygone styles.

It's as close as many hipsters, enslaved to an innate hatred of gender stereotypes, will ever get to being a pole dancer. At ramshackle cabaret nights held in dingy dive bars in the wrong end of town, they clumsily man-handle giant fans lined with ostrich feathers, or pretend not to look awkward as they peel off a 1940s US Airforce uniform to a tinny soundtrack of tea dance music. Making money is a rarity, but that's the downside of life as an artiste, especially one as cultural and subversive as a burlesque dancer.

no.**24**

COMIC STORE OWNER

What sort of person frequents a comic store?

If you said "geek" then you are mistaken.

The correct terminology is "person or persons with a specialised interest." But what kind of persons are to be found in one? Behind the counter, but not necessarily serving people, is the owner. He's pale, with almost translucent skin caused by the fact he rarely ventures outside unless it's to buy a can of Dr. Pepper. He's the big fish in this small, nerdy pond. At the moment he's waiting impatiently for proofs of his self-published autobiography—he's commissioned an underground artist to turn his life story into a graphic novel. It will be sold in the shop in a special glass case. He's convinced it's going to be a huge success. It's his destiny.

His dark hair is sculpted into a pompadour, his blue eyes framed by a pair of thick, black-rimmed glasses. He's the Clark Kent look-a-like with the Superman sized chip on his shoulder. He remembers when it wasn't cool to like comic books, back in the days when he was six years old. "I had the best English teachers in the world," he tells people. "Marvel and DC!" He snorts loudly at his hilarious joke, causing a green bubble of mucus to form in his right nostril, which he wipes away with his sleeve. What he doesn't tell people is that his girlfriend broke up with him because he refused to throw

58   **Comic Store Owner**

away any of his action figures, and because she held a secret suspicion that all those brown cardboard boxes that he has stacked around his apartment actually contain porn, not comic books.

There will be a few youngsters in his shop. Regardless of whether they're 6 years old or 16, they'll be kept a beady eye on by the other customers in case they spoil some of the titles with their gummy, snotty fingers. One patron they won't want to cross is the comic book hipster, who is identifiable by her t-shirt of a flop superhero movie, The Green Lantern for instance, and an oversized woollen hat. Make eye contact and she'll tell you that she liked the original books way before Hollywood got involved and took a giant dump on Hal Jordan.

If you are not a comic book aficionado, then you will no doubt be bemused by the conversations that shoot past you in hushed, urgent tones. Daniel Clowes, Robert Crumb, Neil Gaiman… "Who are these people?" FFS don't say that out loud—you'll be lynched.

FILM MAKER

You don't have to be a hipster to double up as a self-righteous, chin-stroking, over-earnest film maker, but by god it helps.

The spectrum of film assholes ranges from someone who has made a seven-minute documentary about steam punk and uploaded it to Vimeo to an utter bore who spent years at a prestigious film school in New York and has subsequently learnt so much about films that you never, ever, ever want to watch one with them.

You: "So, that was a good movie, huh?"
Him: "To be honest, the director ruined my enjoyment of it by totally discarding the basics of film theory. The narrative was lacklustre, the lighting looked awful, and the shots could have been done by a chimp with a HandyCam."
You: "Oh…"
Him: "And it's not a movie, it's a FILM."

It's not totally dissimilar to going to McDonalds with Jamie Oliver. You'll both have a miserable time, so just try to keep things on their terms, whether that means swapping your kid's daily chicken-nugget fix for a bowl of dry porridge oats to silence the evangelical chef, or attending an ass-aching screening of the film-twat's latest celluloid masterpiece, and then telling him it's got the potential to change the world.

Usually, hipsters like to keep it local as venturing to a new place could mean they get roughed up by some scary kids in hoodies (though not American Apparel ones, they're OK). This might mean their film tracks a local colony of vagrants using an infrared camera so the hobos' after-dark allegiances and amorous moments can be documented in a David Attenborough/*Planet Earth* style, or it could concentrate on an artisinal baker who sells really dreamy rye bread at the local farmers' market.

Whatever the topic, you can be sure it'll be niche. Expect a behind-the-scenes documentary about what goes on during a tour with a hardcore band no one has ever heard of. Think Metallica's "Some Kind of Monster," but starring five skinny kids and a fat drummer you'll never hear of again.

Independent film does have the potential to be glamorous, and for every down-on-his-luck film maker there are at least five broke graduate designers desperate for any sort of exposure. Backstage clips of the goings-on at a fashion show are common-place—for some reason, hipsters, as they recline on leather couches, slowly chewing on olives, just love, love, love to see beautiful, hollow-eyed, malnourished women get their hair and make-up did.

But, the true *pièce de résistance* in a hipster film maker's repertoire will be their "political film" that attempts to overthrow the ruling ideology for something that wouldn't sound out of place in an issue of Adbusters magazine. For instance, a 75-minute attempt to free society from the vice like grip of capitalism with the snappily titled "Buy-limic."

HARDCORE BAND MEMBER

What would be the ideal job for an angry twenty-something who is covered in tattoos from his ears to his toes, has more piercings than fingers, a wardrobe rammed full of wife-beater vests, and a head brimming with unsated teenage angst? Obviously, member of a hardcore band will always feature somewhere near the the top of the list.

Don't dare ask what his band is called, you'll have never have heard of it and it will have broken up and reformed with a new drummer by the time it's getting any hype online.

No hardcore band has ever made a name for themselves by writing songs that concentrate on how lucky they were to have two parents who love them, a big house with a swimming pool, annual snowboarding trips to the mountains, and a private school education. Hardcore lyrics rarely venture far from "don't kick me when I'm down" and "I live with this pain" to "judge me and you'll be judged with my hate." Imagine shouting out the contents of a diary you found in a thirteen-year-old's bedroom, a thirteen-year-old who isn't allowed to go on a camping trip with his friends because he has to go to his grandmother's 80th birthday instead.

Hipsters also like traveling in a pack, meaning the band mentality and touring lifestyle is perfect for them. Late nights, partying, fucking around after midnight in between the bar and a house party, and drinking warm beer are all things that these folk thrive on. The constant stream of bored-looking female groupies, desperately searching for new ways to rebel against their perfectly reasonable parents, are another plus point. The members of the band enjoy nothing more than explaining the inspiration for their numerous tattoos, complaining how much of an asshole their dad is, and how they'll never ever succumb to the ways of The Man. Throw in a musical soundtrack of someone screaming at you with a voice that sounds like they've been forced to dine on sack of gravel since the age of seven, a few shots of tequila, and a skateboard to drunkenly attempt to ollie on and you have the makings of an enchanting evening.

On the flip side, there are plenty of straight-edge hardcore bands who shun all the fun stuff: alcohol, cigarettes, and recreational drugs. Instead they choose to just get a natural high from shouting about being pure and not needing chemicals in their veins to feel alive. "The buzz that self-righteousness can give is better than any line of coke, dude."

The difference between these self-satisfied screechers and their non-abstinent counterparts is that their after-parties suck. Who wants to do shots of water FFS?

ON GLASSES

Up until recent times, glasses were strictly the domain of those who couldn't see very well.

They had their downside. A child who had to wear glasses at school would suffer the embarrassment of their peers calling them "Four Eyes," but this was a small price to pay in return for the gift of sight. However, in the last decade or so, two things came along that would change how we viewed glasses forever: Harry Potter and hipsters. Harry Potter gave hope to geeky kids that one day they, too, might turn into heroic wizards rather than socially awkward comic book readers, but it was the hipster who truly revolutionized glasses. Much like Hitler appropriated the swastika, turning it from a symbol of luck to one of hatred, the hipster took the humble spectacle and transformed it from a practical item into a symbol of total idiocy.

The first hipster to stumble upon the idea of wearing unnecessarily large frames had a genuinely good reason to require a cheap pair of specs. In a time when ugly, thick-framed glasses were strictly the domain of pensioners and pedophiles, a career as a partially sighted graphic designer was proving tricky and certainly wasn't going to pay the bills. So he bit the bullet and shamefully bought a pair of the cheapest glasses he could find. On his first outing into the city, he wore the hood of his American Apparel hoodie up and kept his head down, hoping none of his friends would see. But, in a fortuitous twist of fate, he bumped into a style blogger who took his picture, stuck it on tumblr, and provided the inspiration for tens of thousands of "individuals" to "invent" a similar look themselves. And so the hipster glasses were born.

Following the explosion of idiots with 20–20 vision requiring glasses, manufacturers were tasked with created uglier, larger, thicker frames to suit the myriad requirements of your average hipster. Here are some of the results...

The "I like staying in on a Friday night to bake" pair

At night, she snuggles under a duvet with *Fifty Shades of Glaze*. She is consumed by cakes and while her 50s predecessors vowed to always greet their man with a smile, they didn't have to queue for fifteen minutes at Whole Foods to buy organic flour, did they?

The "I work in the media" pair

Unfortunately for hipsters, since Specsavers started offering dark-framed lenses as part of a buy-one-get-one-free offer, every man and his dog looks like they work for a celebrated creative media agency.

The "I had 'em before Mad Men was cool" pair

If he hears one more person whisper "Sterling Cooper," he'll definitely be a mad man. He wears his frames, vintage Bausch & Lomb, as a tribute to American engineering.

The "I take drugs and wear these in clubs" pair

It's a no win situation—wear these and everyone can see your eyes rolling in their sockets like a couple of marbles in a shoebox or wear proper sunglasses and look like a dick. Stay home or stay sober you Johnny Depp, Gonzo-jerk wannabe.

The "These are original 1950s" pair

Do trends still look as good second time around? Ask that man over there in a weird pair of glasses he paid $600 for—not including lenses.

The pair that inspired a million hipsters

If there is a god, one day ophthalmologists will find the poseur who first started wearing glasses without lenses and burn them at the stake. It'll make the Salem Witch Trials look like Easter.

The "What do you mean? I've always loved Carl Perkins" pair

You might envy how they can wear a neckerchief without looking like a Dexy's Midnight Runners groupie, but rockabilly's eyewear tastes lie somewhere in the no man's land between Dame Edna Everage and Janet Street-Porter.

The "I dream of photographing teenage girls" pair

Dressing like a pervert seems to make acting like a pervert okay, or, at least, expected. Dressing like a pervert photographer, however, doesn't necessarily make your pictures any better. And, from this angle, that picture of her doing that with that is gross.

The "I don't just listen to indie, I like hip hop, too" pair

Wearing a pair of Cazals means he can give a nod to 1980s Brooklyn without having to pick up a can of paint—or learn how to breakdance. His favorite kind of hip hop is the kind that features Chris Martin tinkling the ivories.

INTERNET START-UP ENTREPRENEUR

Jason smiled as he carefully dismounted his fixed-gear bike.

"Hi," he said, smiling and sticking his hand forward as if to instigate a friendly handshake. "Nice to meet you."

But his hand was being thrust towards thin air, he was acting. Today was the day that he was making a YouTube promo for his art gallery—d4gg3r5dr4wng4113ry.tumblr.com.

The backdrop to this short introduction was Chicago's Wicker Park neighborhood. With its laid-back vibe and abundance of cool bars and kooky stores, it summed up everything he loved about life. Plus, there were loads of places to pick up a decaf coffee. He spent a lot of time here: shopping, eating tacos, sinking PBR beers with his buddies, and most importantly, getting ideas for his artworks.

He saw a girl he knew from yoga walk past with a Boston Terrier puppy and couldn't resist flashing her a glimpse of his perfect white teeth. She pretended not to know him.

"Dude! Come on!" grunted Danny, his best friend, gallery co-owner, and cameraman. It had taken him ages to choose the locale for this crucial opening shot, and the longer they left it, the more likely it was that the footage would look crappy—

iPads can be temperamental like that. He really didn't need Jason, with his Obey sweater and limited edition Jeremy Scott Adidas teddy trainers, to become as distracted as his outfit.

"Hi, I'm Jason," he began again. "Proprietor and leader of the Daggers Drawn Gallery. We are a cutting-edge online gallery where you can look at really cool, meaningful paintings, and even buy them, too. All our paints are vegan-friendly— we actually make them ourselves from ancient recipes we found on a website run by the indigenous people of Mexico.

"Every week on Daggers Drawn there is a new exhibition, which is always based on a political or social theme that has inspired me and my collective in the days prior. This week, it's war."

He turned away from the camera, and when he stood back into shot, was wearing a crudely crafted bullet belt. "These bullets," he said slowly, "are made from empty tubs of Yakult. I painted them to make them look like shells.

"They represent not just the futility of war, but the cruciality of recycling. If we lose the eco-war, then our sidewalks will look like a war zone with discarded litter piled up like festering cadavers."

He glanced up at Danny who gave him an eager thumbs-up from behind his gadget. "That's a wrap, bro! International fame and fortune here we come!"

MODERN DANDY

It's hard to describe what makes a "dandy," but iconic Englishman Alan Partridge almost hit the nail on the head.

"It's David Niven. It's Stuart Granger. It's Nigel Havers. The look—imperial leisure. Offset that look with those four summer reliables—hat, cravat, summer spectacles, and, for that touch of class, the Alan Partridge blazer badge."

While the Alan Partridge blazer badge is but a myth, the other items on the suave Norfolk-born broadcaster's list are not; they are wardrobe staples of the modern day gentleman. Like a well-dressed magpie, the modern dandy has a keen eye for all things shiny and usually has a wooden box on his dressing table that is full to the brim with redundant inventions, including collar bobs, money clips, boutonnieres, cufflinks, pocket watches, monocles, and arm bands. He'll scour antiques fairs and flea markets for unusual additions to his tie bar collection, and think nothing of slipping a pair of handmade spatz over his highly polished, high-grade leather shoes.

Monogram is the dandy's ally, and you'll find his initials neatly sewn into his handkerchiefs and the pocket of his silk dressing gown, elaborately engraved on his cufflinks and neatly etched upon his sterling silver cigarette case and matching lighter—unless he's the type to smoke a pipe.

His neck is never bare, and along with a huge collection of ties, he will also own neckerchiefs for casual days by the river or playing tennis with his pals, ascots, cravats for drives through country lanes, sumptuous paisley smoking scarves for when he's enjoying a scotch and a cigar after dinner, dickie bows for jovial afternoons playing whist with lady friends, and luxurious woolen scarves for when winter sets in.

Leisurely hobbies, refined language, impeccable manners, and pretending he's a modern day Oscar Wilde are all just as crucial to the dandy's sense of self as his appearance. A keen eye for finely tailored clothing, from shirts to three-piece suits, socks to ties, waistcoats to overcoats, and all that's in between—including hats and walking sticks—are what truly make a dandy. Whilst his Victorian forefathers might have stuck to a neutral palate, he likes to go wild with textures, patterns, and colors. He'll think nothing of wearing a salmon-pink suit with a green shirt, or a crimson velvet ensemble at Yuletide. The luxe fabric sets off the glow of a snowball cocktail perfectly. "Who says that this tartan handkerchief is too bright for a December morn? Pass me my shoehorn, these spectator shoes are hella' tight!"

A silver comb is kept in his inside pocket at all times, ready to smooth any stray hairs that have escaped his neatly lacquered quiff. Of course, he relies on Hawleywoods products for all grooming matters, whether he enjoys a straight razor shave or cultivating a twiddle-worthy moustache.

Ask a dandy for a pen and you'll be handed a Mont Blanc fountain. Invite him for dinner and expect a hand-typed thank-you letter on high-grade headed paper or a phonecall made from the rotary phone that sits on a little table by his front door—there is no cordless malarkey in his world. To him, he's Gatsby: impeccable, suave, dashing, fun-loving, handsome! But to the casual onlooker in jeans and t-shirts... he's more like a Great Twatsby.

'ZINE MAKERS

Hipsters love to make fanzines because it allows them to use their Macbook for something other than taking digital reels of GPOY photos for their blogs, and surfing the internet looking for rare vinyls and obscure black metal band t-shirts.

You still get the odd 'zine about a band, but they're usually not the twee sort that the Osmonds had dedicated to them in the 1970s. They're more likely to be put out by the band members themselves. Such ventures allow them to illustrate how many girls they've had sex with by putting in double-page spread montages of unaware, post-coital hazed groupies with their faces scribbled out in biro. Or they might just choose to preach about how it's really important to be straight-edge and include some of their favorite on-the-road vegan eats—almond milk and carrot sticks, anyone?

For many writers who can't get a job at a real magazine, making their own fanzine is the closest they'll ever get to their ambition of being the next Cat Marnell. They can write all about drugs and never have to worry about their parents googling them, only for daddy to discover that his regular loans of £50 are either being rolled up… or hoovered up.

'Zine fairs are happening with increasing regularity as more and more people decide that writing a 'zine is their new job—it used to be blogs, but they are sort of samey these days.

Found in the back end of a coffee house, or midweek in some dive bar, regard the dead-eyed twenty-somethings hawking rag-eared copies of their life and times, told and retold by a Xerox machine.

What will you skim read first? "My penis from 15 angles," complete with anatomically correct drawings? The author interned at the Gagosian Gallery, you know. Or do you like that brown-toothed girl's ode to addiction, "Cocaine wraps I have loved and lost?" That guy in the brogues looks like he's never picked up a wrench in his life, but he swears that "Twenty modifications for your fixie bike" is all his own work.

What a surprise, the girl hawking "Short stories from my k-hole" has no idea if she's charging for the 'zine or not. In fact, she doesn't even realize that you're standing there asking her about it. And it goes without saying that the "nouveau riot grrrrrl" title is written by a girl who lives in a plush mews building bought for her by her lawyer parents.

This one looks interesting, "1990 now." It's pages and pages of photographs someone has taken of an iPad showing "The Fresh Prince Of Bel Air," with some captions written underneath. The way that they've juxtaposed the 1990s show with modern-day technology is just so clever.

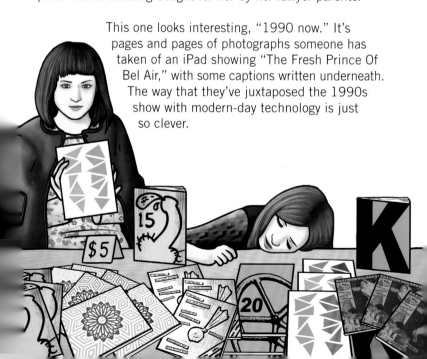

OLD HANGER ON

As much as they might wish they were, hipsters are not Peter Pan.

They don't stay 24 and attractive forever. At some point, their looks are going to fade, their hair will thin and fall out, they will be too old for skinny jeans, and they simply won't know what's cool anymore. The majority of them will accept this gracefully. Maybe they'll have a kid that they can impress in later years with some of their old war stories from warehouse parties and hard drives packed full of jpegs left over from impromptu Instagram photoshoots on roof terraces overlooking the city. Perhaps they will have just forgotten their twenties altogether—ketamine is one hell of a drug.

Or, disgustingly, they might just carry on as if they were still 27 and hot; using slang, sharing memes on Facebook, doing shots, wearing checked shirts, and having casual sexual encounters with anyone that'll put out.

Such characters, left-overs from hipster scenes past, loiter in today's world. You see them, rocking a receding pompadour and handlebar moustache, propping up a bar and staring straight at a 19-year-old's chest. "I'm a photographer," they'll say, taking a sip from their Jack Daniels on ice. "And I could make you a star."

They may very well take photos, but making them a star is unlikely—despite having enough contacts to make it happen. Making them cry is more of a guarantee, as the creepy older dude demands a fix of hot young meat once he's finished snapping his unwitting victim in various stages of undress. There will be more tears when she or he realizes that these shots are now on his tumblr. The fact that he is 50 and has a blog is enough to make him an oddity to people both his age and those who are a fraction of it, and is another reason why he leads his life as that of a lone, predatory, sexually hungry wolf.

And it's not only the men who can't say goodbye to parties with girls with beanie hats and nose rings chopping up lines of cocaine in the kitchen, and rooms crammed full of wide-eyed, pilled-up youths wearing stupid outfits—even though no one has specifically said it's fancy dress. Women are just as guilty.

Aligning themselves as "cougars," they cherry-pick angelic-looking twenty-somethings with slender hips and foppish hair, and install themselves as Sugar Mommies. Whether their virile young charge is a fashion designer, photographer, actor, or artist, they're on hand to fund their materials and living costs—in exchange for the red-hot sex men their own age won't or can't give them. They also demand an invite to all the hottest parties—and not just because they need to make sure some lithe illustration student doesn't steal their man, but because they are addicted to going out, to raising a glass, to living the rock 'n' roll lifestyle, to being in the heart of things, to being the life and soul of the party. Which they are, until someone asks, "So, is that your mom?"

JEWELRY DESIGNER

As a general rule of thumb, if it can somehow be attached to a chain, a hipster will wear it.

This is good news for jewelry designers—both those that have a studio somewhere in East London and those who live with their parents and sell their handmade designs on eBay—as it means that any old tat they find lying around can be sold to someone desperate for a one-off piece of bling. A cotton reel? Make it in to a brooch. A spoon? Make it into hair accessory. A triangle of carpet? That'll make a nice pendant.

Nothing is sacred. Furniture and crockery from an antique dolls house or a yellowing Sylvanian Families play set can be given a fixing and slipped on to a cheap brass chain and sold for a huge profit. Children's toys are the gift that keep on giving when it comes to crafting pendants and earrings—Barbie's shoe makes a nice ear stud, three Barbie heads in a row makes for an interesting hair clip, her torso with "slut" written across it in nail varnish makes for a cool necklace. Plastic zoo animals, dinosaurs, and toy cars can all be worn like a statement piece, especially if they've been spray painted a neon color and then had some Swarovski crystals stuck on.

No effort is too much when it comes to handmade hipster jewelry, with some of it selling for obscene amounts, considering it was found discarded outside the supermarket. As it's cool to look like a devil worshipper these days, many hipsters choose to wear a giant inverted cross and enormous pentagram earrings made from black leather. Or just enormous, metal plate necklaces or anything shiny and owl-shaped. Knuckledusters, spikes, and, of course, moustaches, feature heavily on rings. The latter is especially popular with the kind of girls who like to share Instagram photos that they've tagged "selfies"—which is a vomit-inducing way of saying "self portrait."

But, amongst all the twee pendants and riot-grrrl inspired four-finger bar rings, there has to be an element of irony in there somewhere, and no more so is it found than around the neck of a scenester wearing a Big Mac carton like a locket. Fast food packaging features heavily in pretentious warehouse raves, where an empty KFC bucket on a chain can double up as a place to hide your stash, and girls wear bows in their hair made out of bacon double cheeseburger wrappers from Burger King as if it was the most normal thing in the world.

VEGAN

We are constantly told that the world we live in is heading to hell in a hand cart, so vegans probably deserve some sort of respect.

They are the most moralistic people on the planet. But, when you combine an "I'm better than you as I don't eat cruel foods" outlook with an "I'm better than you as I'm different and artistic and cool" attitude, you've got a recipe for a big dollop of self-righteous tofu.

It's not surprising that of all the world's types of hipsters, the vegan ones are treated with the most disdain. From their spindly limbs to wispy beards, graying vests, and loose-fitting skinny jeans, just one glimpse of them is enough to incite vitriol.

The most important thing in a vegan hipster's life, other than their PeTA membership card, is the compulsory 10lb bag of quinoa that they have in their kitchen. Grains and vegetables make up the majority of their diet, mostly because dairy-free cheese is little more than a rubbery paste and tofu gets boring after about three meals. They churn their own milk by mixing ground almonds and water in a bottle and shaking it until it froths up.

Grains also play an important part in their daily skincare routine. Shunning sweet-smelling cosmetics and bath oils for organic products made of hemp husks, some choose to use a handful of porridge oats and honey instead of a loofah. This can be confusing for small children who, attracted by their breakfast aroma, ask them for a cuddle. Luckily, at knee-height it is impossible for the mites to see the pustules that have returned to their sallow cheeks—chemical-free cosmetics are no match for recurring acne.

As with all hipsters, there is a certain amount of hypocrisy in their actions. They love animals so much that they have totally turned their backs on industrialized farming, yet they are happy to make their beloved pets go against nature and eat a diet as meat-free as theirs.

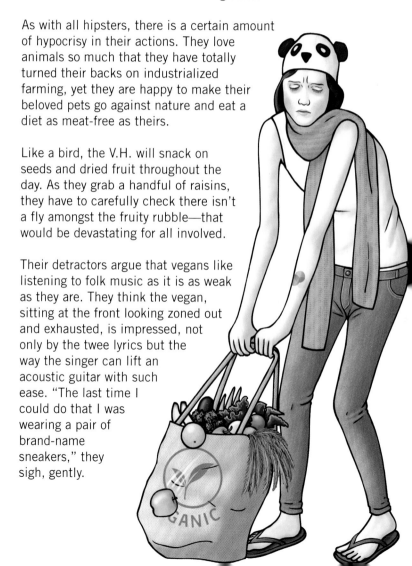

Like a bird, the V.H. will snack on seeds and dried fruit throughout the day. As they grab a handful of raisins, they have to carefully check there isn't a fly amongst the fruity rubble—that would be devastating for all involved.

Their detractors argue that vegans like listening to folk music as it is as weak as they are. They think the vegan, sitting at the front looking zoned out and exhausted, is impressed, not only by the twee lyrics but the way the singer can lift an acoustic guitar with such ease. "The last time I could do that I was wearing a pair of brand-name sneakers," they sigh, gently.

ON HIPSTER HAIRCUTS

Non-hipsters caused a bit of a stink when tumblr became awash with hollow-cheeked young men proudly rocking their "Hitler Youth" haircuts.

Some even went as far as to brand them "Deutschebags." Not that the Kraut-cutted boys in the know gave a shit. Another unlikely style icon is John Travolta. Well, Danny Zuko from *Grease* to be precise. Boys wanting to buy into the greaser/rockabilly trend hold his pompadour in high esteem, and never leave home without a comb and some extra Brylcreem—and an inner voice to assure them that they're cool enough to be a senior at Rydell High.

Girls, however, aren't obliged to cut their hair like a tween disciple of A.H and, in fact, can have a lot of fun with their locks. Some even have so much fun that they cultivate a mane that would make a My Little Pony jealous.

Dip dye, or ombre style as they say in France, is when the tips of the hair are bleached. There are many variations on the theme, obviously—no two hipsters want to look the same, as that's totally against the point of being a non-conformist to an ideal. The tips are colored neon, left yellow and raw, or colored in strips like a raccoon on LSD's tail. Dyeing the hair an all-over color like pink is also popular, as is spending hours

crafting a fade from aquamarine to sky-blue that runs from roots to tips.

For girls, having long hair is the most important thing, and not just because hipster heroine Lana Del Rey has it. Not only does it look better when dip-dyed, but it's also the right length to twist up into a top knot. This is basically a scruffy bun on the top of the head, that lends the wearer a type of nonchalant air. It's also the right length for more elaborate styles, including a "hair bow" in the style of Lady Gaga.

When the preferred styles of he and she reach an inevitable crossroad, it is in the shape of "The Skrillex"—long hair with an extreme undercut on one side that runs from temple to nape. It is the mullet of our times. It is the Billy Ray Cyrus mullet of thirty years from now, the decade's worst haircut. But no one thinks that… yet.

BAR OWNER

You know that nice pub on the corner? Bit of an old man's place but it's got a jukebox and four varieties of nuts?

Yeah, that one with the cheap beer and the darts board. Well, it's been taken over by some twat.

Hipsters love nothing more than getting hold of a perfectly fine—if not slightly stagnant—old pub or bar and giving it a total overhaul. Walls painted, new furniture, new menu, new drinks policy... they love creating a safe place for them and others like them. A place where they can talk about Instagram filters and the new Mumford and Sons album without someone laughing at them.

A place where they can gossip about comic books like seven-year-olds without someone telling them to grow up and start reading newspapers.

"This used to be a pub. I bought it with some inheritance from my grandmother, kicked out the elderly regulars, and installed some spitoons and a strip pole. It's a much cooler place to hang out now. My granny would definitely approve.

"When the old landlord first told everyone it was my pub now, there was one guy who was crying. He was, like, 90 years old. I had to tell him that, y'know, this isn't his scene anymore. Times change, he's had his fun, and now it's time for a new generation to put their stamp on the world. Plus, I really don't want an old codger spoiling the panorama of my new imported Italian marble bar.

"Every Wednesday is open mic night; a guy I know with a bassoon is coming next week. Last time I saw him he was dressed up like Pol Pot. He's so cool, he just does whatever he feels like, y'know? He covered Animal Collective in the style of Justin Bieber once... so funny. And he's so sick on that tuba!"

12 CLUES YOUR LOCAL PUB HAS BEEN TAKEN OVER BY A HIPSTER

1. It serves bloody mary cocktails—but only at weekends as part of the brunch menu.
2. You've never heard of any of the bottled beer. Blue Moon? 312? Where's the Heineken?
3. The inside walls have been painted dark gray or black, or totally papered with oppressive flock wallpaper.
4. There is no ketchup to go with that organic biodynamic burger you spent £15 on for lunch.
5. Peanuts have been replaced with locally sourced organic scotch eggs—at £6 a pop.
6. It gets given a stupid new name, like "The Nun's Whisper" or "The Ebullient Augur."

7. The locals no longer drink there. A pub such as this is no place for anyone over 40 and definitely not for anyone who doesn't have an iPhone.
8. The jukebox is no more and instead the bartenders play "cool music"—this could be anything that you will never hear played on commercial radio.

9. Suddenly the exterior seems to have grown an armor made of bicycles.

10. You see posters for a film night—but before you have time to get excited, realize that the films are thoroughly unenjoyable foreign obscurities like Amasi Damiani's *Un Brivido Sulla Pelle* or Hanna Schygulla's 1966 drama *Katzelmacher*.

11. One Friday night is ruined by a girl crying outside whilst a guy with a moustache and a beanie hat shouts at her about something to do with final projects.

12. There is a new "entertainment" programme: burlesque, folk duos butchering David Bowie, skittles.

POP-UP RESTAURANTEUR

In the same way that blogs have led people to believe that anyone can be a journalist, pop-up restaurants have convinced many that they are chefs.

It's just so easy to have your own pop-up restaurant business. After all, they do it on *The Apprentice* at least once a series. The best thing about manning your own independent kitchen, is that you can make it fit in around your lifestyle.

Want the afternoon off? Wake up early and offer a bespoke breakfast bap near a busy station. Want a lie-in? Have people come over for dinner after applying for a spot around the table using a special hashtag on Twitter.

Any pop-up restaurateur worth their salt will be aware that their meal has to lie equidistant between simple and fancy. For instance, a hot dog bun filled with three frankfurters that make an interesting geometric pattern when sliced in two is a sure-fire winner. "Let people begin their meal with their eyes," they'll enthuse, as they try and get another portable BBQ going, while frantically trying to stuff the supermarket plastic bags into their pockets. If a punter realizes that he hasn't just paid $12 for three especially imported organic German fingerwursts from Nuremburg, but three anaemic looking sausages from a jar of brine, he might ask for his money back. And Tweet about it (god forbid). Just imagine if he knew that was just a wholemeal roll and not a rye doorstop cob from an organic bakery on a tiny farm in the country.

Hipsters like eating at these places as they're edgy and not branded. Finding out where a cult Mexican food truck is parking up that night gives them a good excuse to cycle to the other side of the city to enjoy a tostada and some slimy guacamole. After a quick Instagram of their dinner and checking in on Facebook so everyone knows that they've eaten tostada and guacamole from a food truck miles from their home, they can get back to their MacBooks—to their freshly downloaded new episodes of *It's Always Sunny In Philadelphia*.

DJ

"That looks like my nan's chest," she thought as she looked down at his scrotum.

It was seven in the morning and the last thing she wanted was to be this close and personal to the crepey puce skin of his testes. "Why won't he just fucking cum already?"

She was bored, but he wasn't. And there was no way he'd be ejaculating any time soon. He'd done so much coke he was amazed he hadn't shit his lungs out already. As he lay on his back, biting his lips and sweating, he was having the time of his life. "This," he thought, "is what I do for a living."

Actually, it wasn't. He was a DJ, but getting high and getting blown were just part of the job description.

Every night he'd be out somewhere, playing his CDs to a room of dead-eyed twenty-somethings. He remembered so well when he was the one calling the DJ a twat as he was left in the cold as some sneering idiot queue-jumped, usually flanked by a trio of trashy looking girls. Now he was the twat, and he was loving every minute of it.

The night had been pretty standard. His dealer had been round at about ten. Mevlut was sound, always bringing him the best gear in town. Last night he had announced he had some "Very special chip-chop, ninety per cent pure Peruvian flake." Three grams please!

Getting to the club was a blur. "That line," he thought to himself, "that line absolutely fucked me." The line he took was enormous, and this gear was strong—it had made one of his eyes go bloodshot. "I'm the fucking Terminator!" he'd shouted when he saw himself in the mirror by the bar. "I'm the fucking shit!" A guy in a checked shirt sniggered. "Fuck you!" he'd shrieked. "Fuck you, you fucking nobody, I'm the DJ! You're here because of me!" As a group of people came over to diffuse the situation, he turned on his heels and made his way to the DJ booth. "I'll show you," he muttered to himself.

Wednesday nights were usually quite busy in Williamsburg and tonight was no exception. He played an hour of 90s music, it was ironic and irony is cool. "1995 truly was the peak for electronic music," he thought, as he bent down to take a sneaky bump of that delicious, delicious cocaine.

God it made the Outhere Brothers sound even better!

From his vantage point he could survey the whole dancefloor. Lots of American Apparel hoodies, lots of t-shirts with illegible black metal band logos, lots of vests, lots of checked shirts... That's when he spotted him. That prick from the bar. He was immediately enraged. "He'll fucking pay for making fun of me!" he growled, the toxic powder fully overhauling his sense of reason.

He noticed the bar dickhead wasn't alone. He was with a girl. Long lank blonde hair, ripped tights, smeared make-up, every

bone in her sternum visible. She was a real hipster hottie. He knew what he had to do.

As soon as he handed over the decks to Matty, a guy who played only jungle remixes of 2001 RnB, he sauntered over to the ashen-faced Rapunzel. "Want a line?" he said. He noticed that he couldn't move his jaw much to speak. To her it looked like he had a bit of an overbite. "Yeah," she said. "What is it? K?"

He explained—somehow, his face was seizing up more and more by the minute—that this was the best coke in the city and that he had all the connections as he was basically the scene's most respected connoisseur of class A drugs and he was always getting shipments of incredible gear from around the globe. She said she didn't care. She only wanted K.

"If I told you I had some K at home would you come with me?" he asked through clenched teeth. Minutes later he was dragging her through the club. The guy in the checked shirt didn't bat an eyelid—why would he, they didn't know each other. She had been asking him for drugs when Luke had seen them from the booth.

And now, here he was. On his living room floor with that dickhead's girlfriend. "I win!" he thought, as his body involuntarily spasmed. "I fucking win!"

ON TATTOOS

Just like how seeing a man—or god forbid, a woman—with a tribal tattoo makes you snigger, so will one day the sight of a tattoo on an ageing ex-hipster.

When they had that etching done, it really meant something; it probably earned them kudos on Instagram, and might even have appeared on fuckyeahhipstertattoos.tumblr.com. They got their neck tattooed, it looked so hot—and that J.G. Ballard extract on their inner thigh earned them so much head.

But, in the future, when they're screaming at their kid to stop messing around with the yogurts in the supermarket, or are stopped at traffic behind the wheel of a Volvo, their tattoo will look as dated as the large black designs that stretch like geometric oil slicks across the shoulders, backs, and calves of small town thugs and washed-up skanks in shopping malls across the country.

The most popular tattoo for today's hipster is nautical-themed. From intricately sketched steamers emblazoned across chests, to tiny sailboats on the insides of wrists and anchors on fingers that look like they've been drawn in biro by a bored 15-year-old, the trend for oceanic inklings shows no sign of abating. It is notable that people opt for only certain aspects of life at sea—there is no one that has a sailor clutching his rotting dick after fucking one portside prostitute too many, and a mise-en-scene of a squabble of seagulls taking a mass shit on a pensioner after stealing his lunch is also a rarity, sadly.

It's a bizarre fascination—at the time of writing, there was no need to drop an anchor from the side of a fixed gear bike. And sitting at the counter of a coffee shop drinking a flat white is not comparable to trying to order a beer at a rough port-side bar frequented by Russian longshoremen.

But hipster tats do not start and end at boats, with quotes, shapes, novelty items, and animals all equally likely to be found scratched into the bodies of cool types across the world. But what do they mean? And what sort of person has them?

Nautical

What: Tattoos that wouldn't look out of place on a toothless fisherman or career criminal.
Who has them: Any hipster worth their (sea)salt will endeavor to cover themselves from neck to feet with these watery compositions.
Translation: "I saw this on a blog and thought it looked cool."

Geometric

What: Empty circles, dots, stars, squares, lines, etc.
Who has them: If they have a lot of stars they probably used to be an emo, so see if you can find their old Live Journal account for unlimited teasing ammo.
Translation: "The emptiness and repetitive pattern is what makes it meaningful. God, when will someone understand!"

Animals

What: Realistic sketches of wild beasts like wolves, bears, hawks.

Who has them: Mostly men who dress like weak lumberjacks.

Translation: "I am at one with my instincts, now pass me a chilled locally-brewed beer."

Novelty

What: Moustaches on fingers, pipes or bongs on thumbs, microphones along the length of a wrist.

Who has them: Irritating scenesters—but really the fault lies with the tattoo artist who has encouraged their annoying behavior by fulfilling their lame body art request.

Translation: "I'm cool as I don't take myself seriously— actually I do, so don't judge me, or I will throw my soy latte over you."

Prose/quotes

You can disappear here without knowing it

What: A sentence or two from a depressing poem or cult novel.

Who has them: Someone who isn't on Facebook as they prefer to read out-of-print books.

Translation: "I didn't read the whole book, I just skimmed it until I found a few lines that would look good on the inside of my arm."

One-word philosophies

What: A single word that describes an aspect of their character or appearance, or acts as daily encouragement. Often found on feet, toes, and knuckles for extra impact; sometimes written in a foreign language. Palms of hands are also great places to feature words like "help."

Who has them: Anyone who can label themselves in a matter of letters, e.g. survivor, fighter, believer, kleine, hope, chump.

Translation: "Don't talk to me; read my tattoo and go away."

Latin

What: A Latin phrase indelibly engraved across the chest area, usually found in close proximity to an owl and a scroll. Usually vaguely far-fetched when applied to modern life, e.g. "sero venientibus ossa" means, "those who are late get bones."

Who has them: Serious types who may or may not have checked the accuracy of the motif before undergoing seven hours of excruciating pain in the tattooist's chair. Hipsters who listen to hardcore bands and love nothing more than working up a sweat dancing like an aggressive ape at a sold-out secret show.

Translation: "I'm so serious. And I listen to a lot of bands you've never even heard of before."

sero venientibus ossa

PHOTOGRAPHER

In an ideal world, a hipster would love nothing more than to roam the streets with ten different cameras hanging from their neck like Dennis Hopper in Apocalypse Now, capturing the city in a string of irreverent mise-en-scènes.

Wow! Someone else's graffiti! Look! Thought-provoking scribbles on a toilet door about how this sentence is the only mark the author will ever make on society! OMG! A pug in a onesie. WTF! A girl dressed in a Ninja Turtles t-shirt snorting a line off a Spacehopper at a warehouse party!

However, cycling with all that shutter-candy would cause no end of problems, which is why hipsters absolutely adore Instagram. The Instagram app is the number one reason people of a certain ilk buy an iPhone. It's a magical way of making any photograph look interesting and cool, is the easiest way to come across as artistic and talented, and creates the best, most compelling images ever. The chances are that if Robert Capa was still alive, he'd want to go back in time so he could take photos of the D-Day landings using just this handy app (probably). But, there are some people for whom deliberating between Earlybird and Toaster effects is not enough. Despite the unstoppable rise of digital photography, there are some who remain loyal to the nuances and uncertainty of analogue photography.

Worldwide, people experiment with expired films and long-forgotten camera models, then share the results on Lomography forums and on Flickr. The more blurred the image is, the more inappropriate the saturation of its colors, the more over-exposed it is, the higher the kudos to the photographer.

Regardless if the tool is a cell phone, a Diana mini-camera from the Lomography shop, a beat-up medium-format model, or an original Olympus Trip, the aim is to create ethereal, bleached-out photos that look like a forgotten moment from the family album, or an unseen still from a David Lynch movie. However, there are plenty of people out there for whom photography is seen as an AAA pass to the scene's hottest parties, and hottest revelers.

They aspire to be Mark Cobra Snake, the unofficial Hollywood hipster photographer who counts his A-list subjects as friends. They dream of being Tyler Shields, the skater-turned-artist who persuaded Lindsay Lohan to let him cover her in fake blood. They dream of taking pictures of a girl in her aunt's original 1970s poncho as she checks her too-dark eyebrows in the reflection of her iPad, and then uploading them to Facehunter. Modern day photography: it's all about the posing, baby.

BLOGGER

Some hipsters treat their blog with the same esteem as they do their MacBook or fixed gear bike.

Queuing for a coffee, you can often overhear them discussing possible themes and backgrounds as if they were picking new wallpaper or a couch for the living room.

"I'm not sure if I should just pay $49 for that cool tumblr theme, or ask Brad if he can write some CSS code for me." "It's a tricky one, as it has to look cool." "Yeah, it totally has to. It's crucial that it looks cool."

"Managing" a blog can become all engulfing; it's an individual's virtual coat of arms, their shop window in the global cyber mall, their chance to show people all over the world how refined—yet underground—their interests are.

Blogs also allow aspiring young hipsters stuck in out-of-the-way villages or brain numbingly lame towns to live their lives as if they aren't the local oddball who wears his sister's skinny jeans and a musty leather jacket he got from a thrift store. They can pretend that they are really good at skateboarding, or have tattoos, or read graphic novels with a print run of 10, or know pretty girls with elaborate dip dyes and French Bulldogs, or interesting graphic designers who regularly brunch in Williamsburg.

Depending on their personal level of narcissism, bloggers are content to post up a mixture of photos of their outfits, their favorite memes, some obscure music videos, pictures of baby animals, the odd rant about consumerism and the decay of society, or some other vehement ramblings about the state of their relationships.

However, a large chunk of bloggers take it much more seriously and actually think they're journalists. Their vanity levels scale new heights as they attempt to transform themselves into the online world's most relevant music writer or fashion commentator.

Opposite: The reality of blog life

Like a frightening statuette of a snake eating itself tail first, it is impossible to know who is more ostentatious: the interviewee or the interviewer. They track down unknown-but-underground DJs from Europe, or a hat designer who makes millinery using only cling film, and milk transcriptions from them that run over pages and pages, but reveal nothing. Nevertheless, they are diligently typed up and shared with approximately six readers, and maybe a few more if the author tweets it using some snappy hashtags.

In their mind, the hipster blogger is doing something really important: acting as a gatekeeper for new movements and ideas; heralding change in the arts world; discovering the next big thing. In reality, they are usually just posting up pictures and MP3s of someone else's graft—this is particularly true for street art blogs, which are just a string of Instagrammed tags, murals, and throw ups. The emotions, woeful poetry, and hackneyed ideas that accompany these stolen snaps, however, are all their own work.

The most popular blogs are ones where there are multiple opportunities to make fun of people. Being mean about people who haven't got the chance to defend themselves never gets old.

Opposite: The fantasy of blog life

INTERN

The Native Americans understood that the route to adulthood was not an easy one.

The Mandan tribe's coming-of-age ritual was particularly brutal, involving hook hanging, having splints driven into limbs, three days of fasting, passing out from loss of blood, and, finally, the sacrifice of a pinkie finger.

Similarly, young wannabes must perform at least one internship before becoming a fully-fledged hipster.

They apply for work experience at "cool" establishments in their droves, firing out emails even faster than they fire out tweets about the latest Grizzly Bear album or the cupcake they are about to eat. They aspire to be making coffee and answering phones at an independent publishing house, design agency, boutique PR company, magazine, record label, fashion house, avant-garde theatre, or record store.

They relish every moment of their tenure, thinking this is their taste of what their future could be like… and they're right. While they think they are getting a first-hand view of the banter, freebies, parties, and general shenanigans that come from working in the creative industries, really they are just discovering that if they want to do a cool job, then they'll have to do it for next to nothing, or for free.

The youngster is inevitably given "a really important project"—this could be listening to demos and entering the

details in a spreadsheet, or stacking magazines in date order, or clearing out a cupboard, or reorganizing shelves—but to the intern it's like they've been entrusted with someone's life. They don't realize until they are much older and have had their spirits broken by working life that really they were just doing the menial jobs no one can be bothered to do.

Internships also allow the young, green students to learn the hipster code from seasoned pros. For several weeks they will be immersed in the subculture, despite perhaps not even

realizing it. Being sent to fetch coffees teaches the young protégé how to interact with baristas and about all the different combinations that can be made with soy milk and coffee. The office being run down and cheap starts them wearing a scarf indoors all year round. A steady stream of contributors, photographers, models, and artists gets them used to making ridiculous small talk.

And this training continues outside of the workplace as the intern develops a sense of self-righteousness that will alienate their friends and have people muttering that they're a twat. This could be because they've started wearing glasses despite having 20/20 vision, or because they suddenly won't eat McDonalds as it's "too corporate."

The intern will inevitably big up their responsibilities to the point of lying. They'll claim they make their important, cool bosses laugh, are styling a fashion shoot, boast that they are allowed to write an album review for the website, or have been put in charge of marketing, when really they have just been sent to the printers to pick up some flyers.

They will omit the dullness of their ten-hour working day, never mentioning that they were made to traipse across the city to get their boss a Korean bubble tea, had to write addresses on 1000 envelopes as there were no labels,

or were made to spend an entire day cold calling.

The full time job at the end of their stint never comes to fruition. Once their friendly editor has run out of ideas for menial tasks that no-one else is prepared to do, the dejected intern is forced to try their luck somewhere else. And just as cheap sluts get passed from one football star to another, good interns are passed from company to company, getting screwed over and over again.

But at least they're getting screwed over in a cool way, right?

FASHION EDITOR

Have you ever wondered how trends start?

He was used to all eyes being on him, as one of Williamsburg's most adored fashion editors, he was always all over the Internet. He was so famous that he didn't even have to tell the staff at Verb Cafe on Bedford what he wanted to drink—they knew he wanted a soy latte, and even brought it to his regular table, right by the window.

He liked that spot; people watching was one of his greatest sources of inspiration, and he liked to think that he also inspired people. Inspired people to dress well, take care of their hair, and pay attention to personal grooming. It had taken him a long time to get his moustache equal on both sides, and he also ensured that he never allowed a monobrow to sprout between his thick blonde eyebrows. "Details, people!" he crowed.

No one had rolled up their chinos before he did, and no one had even dreamed of teaming them with Nikes until he had. He was quietly confident that he was the best dressed, and most influential man in Brooklyn. His social life was full with dinners, drinks and exclusive parties, his mailman exhausted from delivering him parcel after parcel of one-off designs and couture samples. Life was good!

Well it was until March 1st 2013. He returned home from a really exciting lunch at a new Mexican-themed sashimi bar to find that there had been a disaster at his home. His bedroom was awash with sewage. The toilet in the upstairs apartment had ruptured and filth had seeped through the ceiling, soaking his style/sleep chamber from corner to corner. Writing about fashion might mean lots of freebies, but sadly home insurance isn't something you get in a goody bag. He could have paid for home insurance but decided to buy a Tom Ford suit, instead. But now that suit, that glorious example of modern tailoring, was defecated by his neighbor's foul-smelling waste.

He turned and ran from the scene, his hand clasping his mouth as he gagged for air. He gagged hard, trying to make himself sick and undo those miso tortilla chips he had just nibbled on. This was god punishing him for eating carbs, he rued.

He sat on the stoop and lit a cigarette. Tomorrow he was being interviewed by Hypebeast. What was he going to wear?! He considered tweeting an SOS but decided against it, instead waiting until night fell to put his plan into action.

His hands stank of shit. He'd tried his best to clean up the mess, but it was gross and he was too upset to really get too stuck in to it. He sprayed them again with cologne before putting on a dark jacket and heading out into the dusk.

He stopped outside the clothing bank, and took a deep breath as he looked around for any witnesses. He felt terrible for what he was about to do, but knew that he had no other option. He hoisted himself up on an overturned crate and stuck both arms in to the shoot of the clothing bin. "These garments are for the needy," he muttered. "And right now, there is no one needier than me!"

As he turned around, he was met with a flash and the tell-tale "ca-shus" sound of an iPhone. He'd been caught. As fast as he could he ran back to his apartment, wishing his Jeremy Scott winged trainers would carry him as fast as Hermes' similar sandals—that's Hermes the Greek god, not the fashion house. After an uncomfortable night's sleep on the couch with a halo of potpourri around his head, he managed to piece together a good enough outfit for his meeting from his bag of stolen clothes. A pair of high-waisted jeans and a t-shirt with a koala formed the bulk of it, and he wore a thick duffel coat over the top.

Walking to the L Train, he noticed something strange. A queue of people at the clothing bank, each of them armed with an eco-friendly canvas bag. They were waiting for their turn to dig through the bin and find a new addition to their wardrobe.

His phone beeped—Twitter. There it was a picture of him, raiding the bin last night with "#NXT TRND" typed on the bottom. He had become a meme. He had started a trend. And Jesus wept (as did the charities who own the clothing bins across New York).

FASHIONISTA

Trudging to the supermarket is not a fashionable event—unless you're a hipster.

To them, the aisles are commensurable with a catwalk, the overhead lighting, the hush of the crowds, the atmosphere that screams "Buy! Consume! Want! Have!"

Ah, the slave to fashion, so easy to spot in her perilous Jeffrey Campbell studded Lita ankle boots and heart shaped Lolita-style sunglasses. Her legs, sausaged into wet-look leather leggings, serve to only highlight just how little of her wages is spent on nutrition. Her upper half wears a t-shirt with two giant upside down crosses over the nipples, and an oversized sheepskin coat. A beanie hat hides hair that hasn't been washed for several days—she's been at a wild party somewhere in a basement—at least she thinks she has.

An alternative to leggings are a pair of tiny denim shorts or a long net skirt with a smaller opaque skirt beneath—neither are particularly practical. But hey, isn't that what fashion's all about? "Mom jeans"—high-waisted and really unflattering—are also held in high regard.

While a lot of hipster outfits could pass for a hairball spat out by the early 1990s, there are other ways they like to dress depending on what they do for a living. Stylists will think nothing of wearing a sequined catsuit, and will happily pair it with a child's backpack. It's as if they like knowing that for all the evil looks they're getting as they walk along the road, there is a flaccid Barney on their back shooting back daggers with his large, plastic eyeballs. Meanwhile a barista will wear some friendship bands they picked up while backpacking through South East Asia when they were 19, as it reminds them of why it's so important to only drink sustainable coffee. Regardless of their job, a pair of lensless black-rimmed spectacles completes any outfit.

Popular unisex items other than skin tight jeans and American Apparel hoodies include checked shirts, faded band t-shirts, leather satchels, OBEY sweatshirts, vests, baseball caps, oversized cardigans, plimsolls, Saudi Arabian shemagh scarves, enormous Nike trainers, Russian trapper hats, trilbys, and Doc Marten boots.

Perhaps this is cause for jealousy between the sexes, but girls can truly go to town with accessories. The fairer of the species love to stuff fake flowers in to their boots, or wear them like a crown around their top knot. They probably think they are a modern day ambassador for the spirit of Woodstock, but their Casio watches always betray their era, as do their iPhones, which are always to hand in case they need to tweet something ironic, or take a photo of themselves in any sort of reflection and put a filter on it that makes it look yellow. They are also partial to headbands, ear cuffs, bangles, and enormous hinged-finger cuff rings that wouldn't look out of place on a Norwegian black metal band.

Basically, they're walking a fine line between embellishment and over saturation, but they #DGAF.

ASPIRING NOVELIST

Ever since I was a born I have wanted to write a novel.

People don't believe me when I say this, but when I was removed from the safe haven of my mother's abdomen (I was a C-section baby) I reached out and grabbed the doctor's pen. It's like I understood why I had been born. I had been born to write.

Since then, I have always thrived on absorbing stories, ready to reveal at a later date. I have found solace in the day-to-day romanticism of daily life. The sound an egg makes as it is cracked against an omelette pan. Noting the subtle nuances that creep through the seasons, transforming the leafy boulevard that I grew up on from a sepia still life to an explosion of summer blossoms, and back again. Relishing comfort through change, and noting down how it made me feel in one of many notebooks.

After witnessing eighteen of these cycles, eighteen consecutive years of Christmas lights after pumpkins after flowers after Easter bunnies, I packed a suitcase and headed to Portland, Oregon. I brought little with me in the way of possessions—my spectacles, some smartly tailored trousers, a plaid shirt, and a typewriter given to me as a passing present by my maternal grandmother.

When she presented me with the 1936 Underworld Four Bank, neither of us could speak. But I knew why she was handing me this. She understands my passion for storytelling and knew that I must be able to write whenever the moment takes me. I could be on a bus, or sitting at a friend's house, or at the cinema—inspiration doesn't discriminate. When I have an idea, it must be captured in ink as soon as possible and my typewriter is the best tool for that.

And here I sit, seven years later, with only the rat-a-tatting of the typewriter and my thoughts for company. Portland has so many coffee shops I never have to visit the same one twice, which is so important for a writer. You need a constant evolution within your environment, like on Acacia Avenue where I grew up. But I suppose Tiny's is my favorite—and not only because I hope eating one of their world-famous voodoo donuts will help inject new life in to my budding narrative.

When I get home to my apartment, I file the papers I have typed up that day in a large leather-bound book I found on Etsy. Then I either relax by reading some Nietzsche, or check Twitter and Facebook on my MacBook, or play Robot Unicorn Attack on my iPad. Apple products are for downtime, my typewriter is for the nitty-gritty real life shit. My typewriter is for my book, my *raison d'être*.

STREET ARTIST

Graffiti hasn't been caught in a state of flux since the late 1980s.

And no, *Beat Street* isn't a representation of where things are at now.

In today's world, graffiti has been over taken by its more accessible, cuter, wittier cousin Street Art as the edgy-vandalism du jour. Some of the scene's most lauded artists, Banksy, Eine, Shepard Fairey, Sweet Toof, and AEON can command thousands for their pieces.

Giant letters, stenciled sketches of children with guns, owls with hypnotic eyes, enormous teeth, Andre The Giant's grimacing face... art critics can't get enough and there are now more pieces in swanky galleries than on the streets so they don't have to worry about being barged into by riff-raff, while trying to decipher and absorb the hidden meanings behind the garish colors and stylized lettering.

Over the last decade, street art has become a part of the tapestry of cities across the world, with many scenester nerds making pilgrimages to the most famous pieces, Instagramming the peeling paper, putting a bleached filter on the chipping paint, looking serious and reflective next to a fading Banksy.

Easy money? Not working full-time? An excuse to stick two fingers up at the establishment? Adoration from peers? No wonder so many hipsters are muscling their way in.

Bearing in mind that most of them moonlight as graphic designers, churning out a few stickers after work or creating a poster with an ironic design and an existential statement is simple. Designing a picture using a character they haven't necessarily created themselves is even easier. And being "funemployed" means late nights spent sneakily sticking them all over the cool end of town isn't a problem—all they have to do the next day is return to the scene of their crime and take some photos they can post on tumblr.

The hipster street artist is identifiable by dirty hands, a scruffier than usual appearance, and the inability to make eye contact. He's terrified that he'll be arrested and his family will find out that their darling son has grown up to become a vandal.

Nevertheless, he always has a back pocket full of stickers and a marker pen with him in case he sees an opportunity to scrawl his tag or write a curse. To him, his environment is a blank canvas, so whether he's at a house party, bar, doctor's waiting room… they are all decent spots for a bit of impromptu art.

Sadly, the hipster street artist's calling card isn't always an insightful phrase or cute cartoon. Pity the poor people of Williamsburg who have seen their local area besieged by a guy who tags "Dickchicken"—and accompanies it with a stencil of… Yup, a chicken with a phallus instead of a face. What the cluck.

RETRO TECHNOLOGY PERSON

They'd be lost without their Macbooks and smartphones, but on the whole, hipsters pine for simpler times.

They miss the days when they had to sit poised by a cassette player ready to press record the moment they heard the opening bars of their favorite song. They reminisce about the hours they spent playing Duck Hunt on the NES, and the adrenaline of having a two-night window to watch a video tape of a film that was released at cinemas eight months prior. They look at life through rose-tinted Wayfarers—which is strange considering most of them are too young to really remember the 1990s.

Anyone who sees the 1990s as some sort of magical time when people dressed like Blossom or Kurt Cobain and listened to Pearl Jam, Ini Kamoze, and The Spice Girls needs a wake-up call. The only positives about the decade were that Facebook was just a twinkle in Mark Zuckerburg's eye, and there was no such thing as email—it meant life was spontaneous and work was left at the office. Plus there were more magazines as the industry hadn't had its guts ripped out by blogs.

Ironically, it's because of the Internet that these kids crave old-fashioned technology so much. They fork out hundreds for a working Super Nintendo and five cruddy games that they need to empty of dust every hour or so, and devote months searching out a rare Aiwa HS-JX505 Walkman so they can listen to their downloaded MP3s on tape—just ten at a time, mind.

They are "interested in" analogue photography, but instead of buying a decent SLR camera, pick up a clunky Nikon that will prefer to eat their expensive film rather than take grainy, red-eyed snapshots. Similarly, they can't quite get their head around the idea that an iPhone app that takes pictures in a papery-looking frame is more efficient than a Polaroid camera. They get into fierce bidding wars on eBay, hoping that this rare package of 600 film will still work despite being eight years out of date. When a picture develops as a brown smear, they still try to pass it off as proof of their artistic merit.

Delusion is the life force of the retrospective hipster. When their friends gloat about getting a high score on Angry Birds, retro hipster pulls out their battered Nokia 5110 and brags about how good they are at Snake. "My phone has changeable covers too," they smirk, before showing off a pixellated drawing of a cock that was sent circa 1999—sexting 1.0.

INDIE BAND

Hipsters are fickle.

That's why you might know a guy who is so obsessed with The Libertines he will argue until he's blue in the face that Pete Doherty's poetry is a dogma for modern living instead of the ramblings of a junkie… but then when you see him four years later he's only listening to a bluegrass band who only ever played half a gig outside a boarded up gun shop at SXSW. Furthermore, he'll deny he ever liked British music, and that his ears have been tuned to the sounds of Appalachia since he was eight years old when he bought his first country vinyl from a strange pensioner wearing a bolo tie at a flea market in Aberdeen.

When these types decide to form a band, it seems like a world-changing decision. Imagine how good they'd look in photos with all their cool haircuts and shiny conker-brown brogues and rolled-up jeans held up with braces! However, most bands break up before even releasing an EP as egos clash, feelings are bruised, and agendas are challenged. This sometimes works in their favor though, as it can potentially give the band mythical status—the band that was so amazing it broke up after a week. The world wasn't ready then, but it might be now they have a new singer and a cute Norwegian girl with a fringe playing keytar—man the way she rocks that Yamaha SH-10 is really sexual, and the two chords she knows sound great.

The quest to be the most obscure person in the room means that it's becoming increasingly hard to find a band with a traditional guitar/bass/drums formation—it's more likely to be ukulele, bongos or timpani, and bassoon, with some added percussion for good measure. Where once it would have been strange to see two girls with a triangle and a pair of maracas tip-toeing through a nine-song set in the back room of a pub, this is now quite normal as twee and esoteric collide to create something really horrible.

If the terrible compositions that they are trying to pass off as songs don't bore you, an in-depth chat about their "influences" will. For every seven bands, genres, record labels, or ragtime compositions of Scott Joplin that you've never heard of there will be a reference to a shitty now-defunct band like Menswear, Good Charlotte, The Lighthouse Family, Shampoo, or The Cardigans. They will probably also say they're "in love with" the music of Paul Simon and Bob Dylan, or whichever one of them is "the dead one." Every hipster claims to like The Beach Boys, even if secretly they think Brian Wilson is a doddery old fool.

If the band manages to control their individual sense of self-importance long enough to make it to an established act stage, then their dream is to tour with Vampire Weekend, Silversun Pickups, Animal Collective, fun., or Grizzly Bear. Imagine sharing a crate of PBR and talking about Ernest Hemingway with those guys in the back of a van! WILD.

Cupcake Baker

If Stepford made hipsters they'd be the cupcake-baking brigade.

Inspired by brain-numbing sitcoms like *2 Broke Girls*, gaggles of young ladies are taking their Etsy mentalities and putting them to work in the kitchen, turning what was once a cheap bedsit into a hardcore baking hub. Obviously they wear an apron they made themselves when measuring out the hand-milled organic flour.

A recent audit of the Internet revealed there are now more blogs about cupcakes than there are porn sites, as home baking slowly ebbs away interesting and useful content one edible grain of glitter at a time.

The more outrageous the gateaux, the more kudos and repins on Pinterest it receives. Organic elderflower cordial buttercream, rainbow sponges, individual cheesecakes with a white chocolate horn so it looks like a unicorn, and peanut butter-inspired icing are the norm. Hipster imagery cut from fondant icing also adorns many of the sweet treats, with iPhone app logos, old video-game characters, tattoo art, moustaches, and beards all making baking aficionados squeal in sugar-fueled ecstasy.

So she can still comfortably slip into her skinny jeans, the cupcake hipster sells the majority of her wares at farmers' markets, independent coffee shops, and vintage clothes pop-up shops. The bohemian baker considers it perfectly reasonable to charge $10 a cake, and so do her customers, who struggle to decide if they love the cupcake's homemadeness more or less than they love the sweet little hand-printed toile bag it's sold in.

The hipster home baker is always busy, making stacks of cakes for weddings, christenings, magazine launches, events raising awareness for bulimia, and recycled paper envelope openings. When it comes to decorating her muffins of smiles and happiness, her inner eight-year-old is allowed to run amok. She traps the cake in a tomb made from chocolate spread, and then adorns it with marshmallows, edible glitter, marzipan animals, chopped nuts, and an inch of buttercream—which may or may not have been dyed an acrid shade of pink.

One day hipsters will be identifiable by their toothless grins after all this sugary indulgence catches up with them. And as the Daily Mash website points out, "Cupcakes will not plug the gaping chasm where your soul used to be."

CRAFTER

Just as the ancient Romans convened at the Forum, hipsters barter and trade on Etsy, which is sort of like a twee version of eBay.

On Etsy there is no need to worry that the Fendi handbag you just bought is fake, as most of the products up for grabs have been designed and made by "craftspeople" and are certainly not branded.

Anything and everything that is hand sewn and useless is available. A doily for your pug's bowl, a screen-printed tote bag with an anti-consumerist slogan, jewelry made from pasta, vomit-inducing illustrations reading "I'm not a hipster, I just dress like one," odd numbers of vintage doorknobs, and cross-stitched portraits of Barack Obama are ten a penny. Similarly, there is an abundance of "shabby chic" furniture—most of which looks like it has been retrieved from a skip outside a dead pensioner's house and given a haphazard coating of pistachio green paint.

When your package arrives from Etsy, you will probably notice that everything about it has been handmade somehow—even the personalized thank-you card that is hand-stamped with a self-carved potato and homemade concoction of vegetable juice ink. They really believe they can make a living out of this.

The Etsy hipster thinks the world would look better if it was covered in a sheath of crochet, and is part of a "guerrilla knitting" collective. These "yarn bombers" cycle around cities looking for trees to strangle with a colorful straightjacket they have made from sustainable, organic yarn. "Street art isn't just for the boys!" they coo, as they document each "bomb," using Hipstamatic to take photos to put on their tumblr.

A visit to their house is like a trip to a junk shop, or the late 70s. Apart from the obligatory MacBook, there will be nothing modern in their abode, unless of course they have just chosen to hide it with a special crocheted cover. Their crockery will be chipped and old, or made from earthenware by a girl who thinks it's ok to wear a bandana that she has made from a discarded wedding dress. The brown glaze the plates are coated in make them look like they are covered in a rubbery layer of old gravy. None of the cutlery is from the same set. As you tuck into a delicious organic lunch, which will no doubt be a mix of quinoa and grated carrot, the Etsy hipster will wax lyrical about how they wish to live in a commune that functions upon the principles of cottage industry. They are blinkered to the realities of early twentieth-century working patterns which saw people force themselves blind as they hunched double for twenty hours a day in a gloomy, draughty shack making lace for a pittance.

The majority of these crafty hipsters are female. Usually they have taken to selling handmade trinkets and scarves online following the birth of their first child, Atticus, or because their degree in Human Sciences has got them absolutely nowhere. Making their own clothes means they are stuck in a permanent state of frumpiness, and their authentic 1950s cat-eye spectacles make them look like one of the girls the T-Birds ignored in *Grease*.

WANNABE HIPSTER

The one thing that hipsters hate more than globalization, intensive farming methods, and TV programs made by Simon Cowell are people pretending to be hip.

And, similar to how a shark can smell blood, they can sniff out a phony from a mile away.

The spurious scenester will try their utmost to fit in—and this is usually the cause of their downfall. They'll interrupt a conversation about the latest EP release from Triangle Records to proclaim, "Yeah, Steve Angello, he's a genius."

They accessorize any outfit with a rolled-up copy of Vice which they carry nonchalantly under one arm. However, their outfit will not be second-hand or vintage, but rather be made up of brand new clothes that are designed to look old. The hipster will be horrified that their new acquaintance's outfit was not pillaged from their grandparents' house, their spectacles not inherited from a long-dead aunt but from Specsavers. Neat stitching and an absence of worn, threadbare areas—as well as not smelling musty—is always a telltale sign of a poseur, and a scenario that has the potential to make a serious hipster wince.

Those serious about protecting their local dickhead community will lay down a virtual assault course while trying to ascertain if this newcomer is legitimate. They'll lay word traps to find out if they were a fan of MGMT before the release of Kids, and will root out whether to them, "JT" is Justin Timberlake, or JT Leroy, the literary hoax/cult author.

Further scorn will be poured on their claim should they reveal that they are "totes into conspiracies" after reading *The Da Vinci Code*, or any book by Dan Brown. Everyone knows actual conspiracy theory sources are dismal spoken word nights, badly organized peace rallies, and poetry slams.

The pretender will lie about their pretentious interests but be caught on the back foot—perhaps being seen putting an aluminium can in a regular rubbish bin, or drinking a Starbucks coffee. Not recycling or having any sort of eco-conscience is sacrilege to the average hipster, and will immediately alert them that there is a charlatan in their midst. In that case, they'll probably just ignore you for being totally uncool or snigger that you're a PZ (philosophical zombie) until you open your own coffee shop or tell them that you're a professional screen printer and want to make a zine with them.

INDEX

ACKNOWLEDGMENTS

Thank you to all my friends (and foes) who inspired me while writing this book. Don't be pissed off with me, take it as a compliment.